Playdates with Dragons
by Cyan Jenkins
Images and Ideas are copyright
by Cyan Jenkins

First Printing 2018 by Lulu
ISBN: 9781387512027

Playdates

with Dragons!

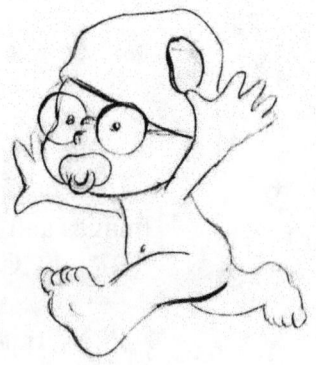

This compilation of sketches
started as an Inktober challenge.
I drew one sketch a day for the
whole month of October and because
I love Dragons, and my boys,
they just started slipping into the
sketches more and more.
October may be over, but my
drawings of Dragons and kids arent.
Enjoy the art!

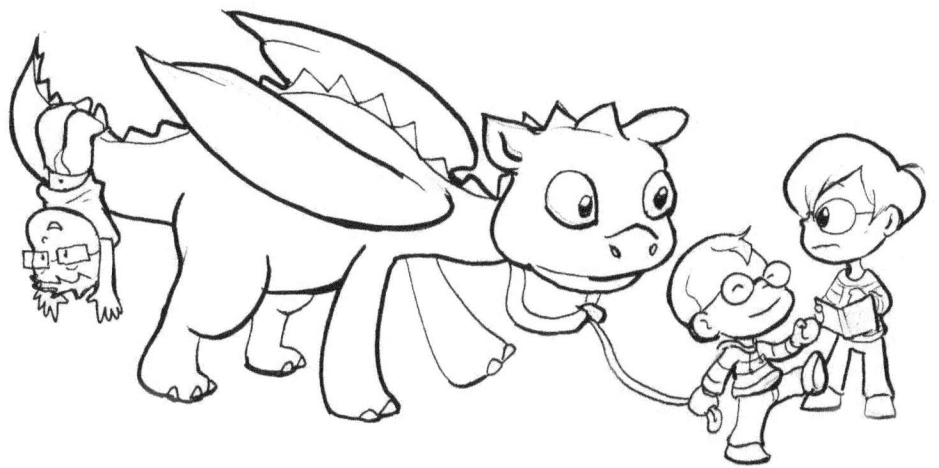

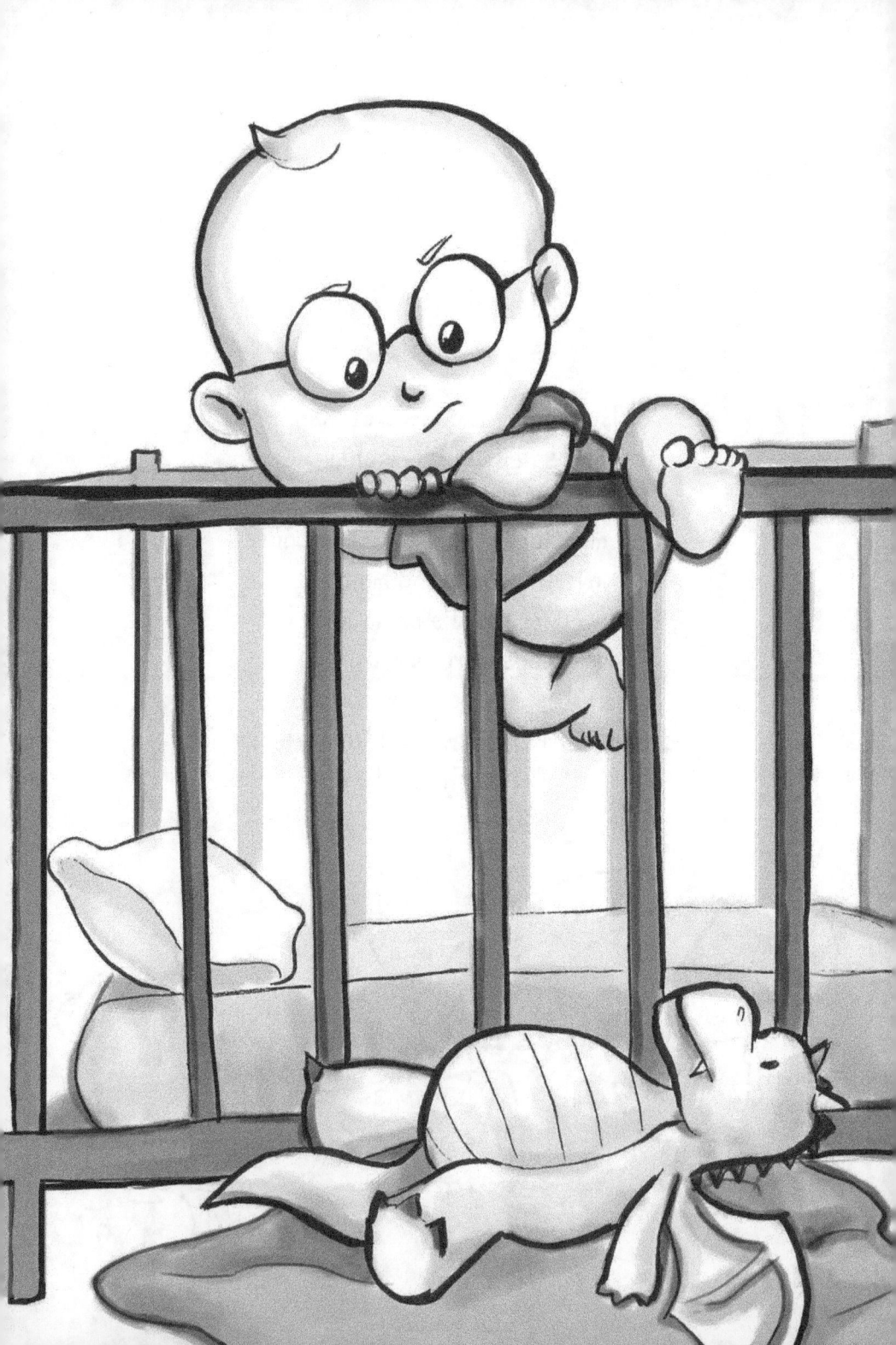

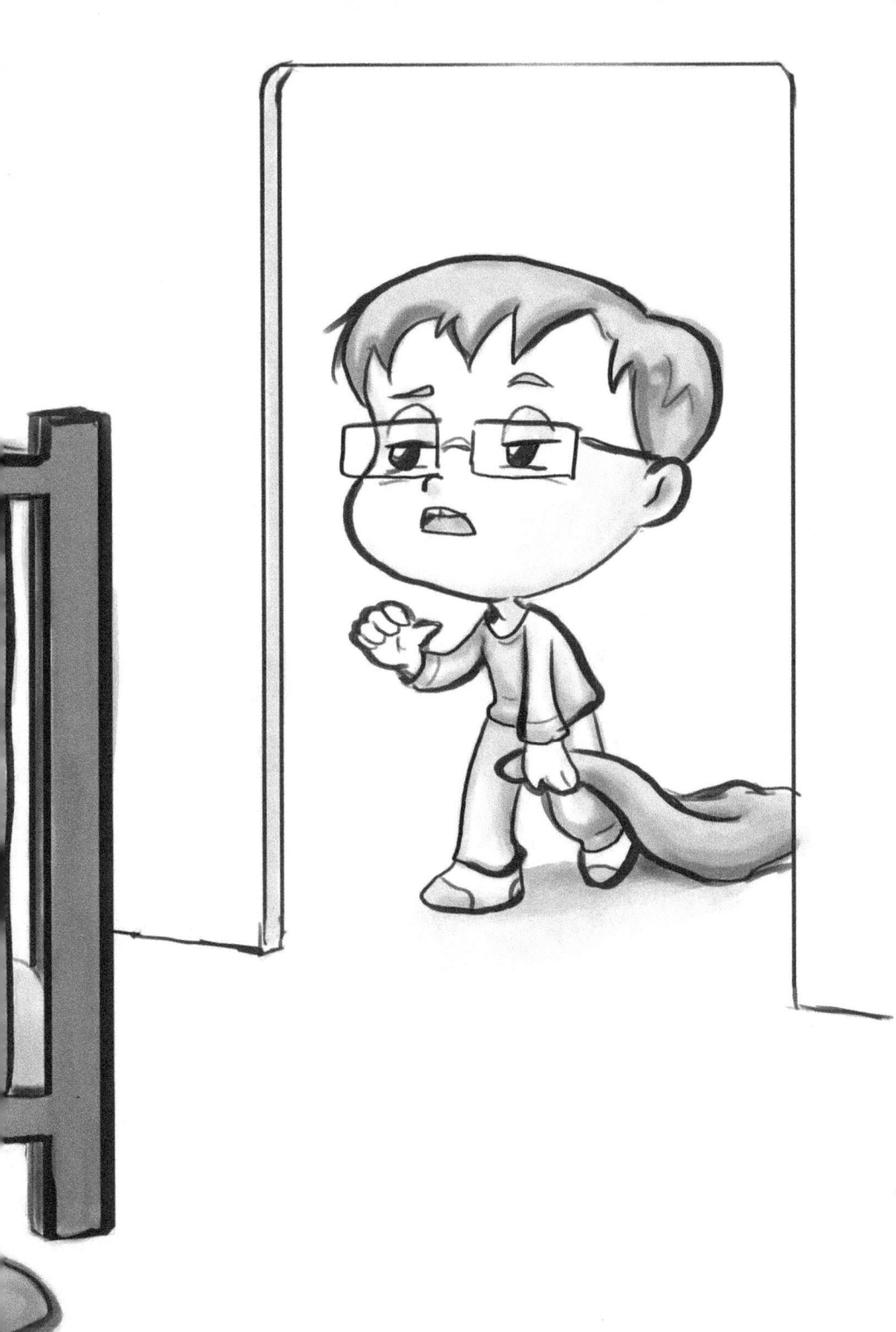

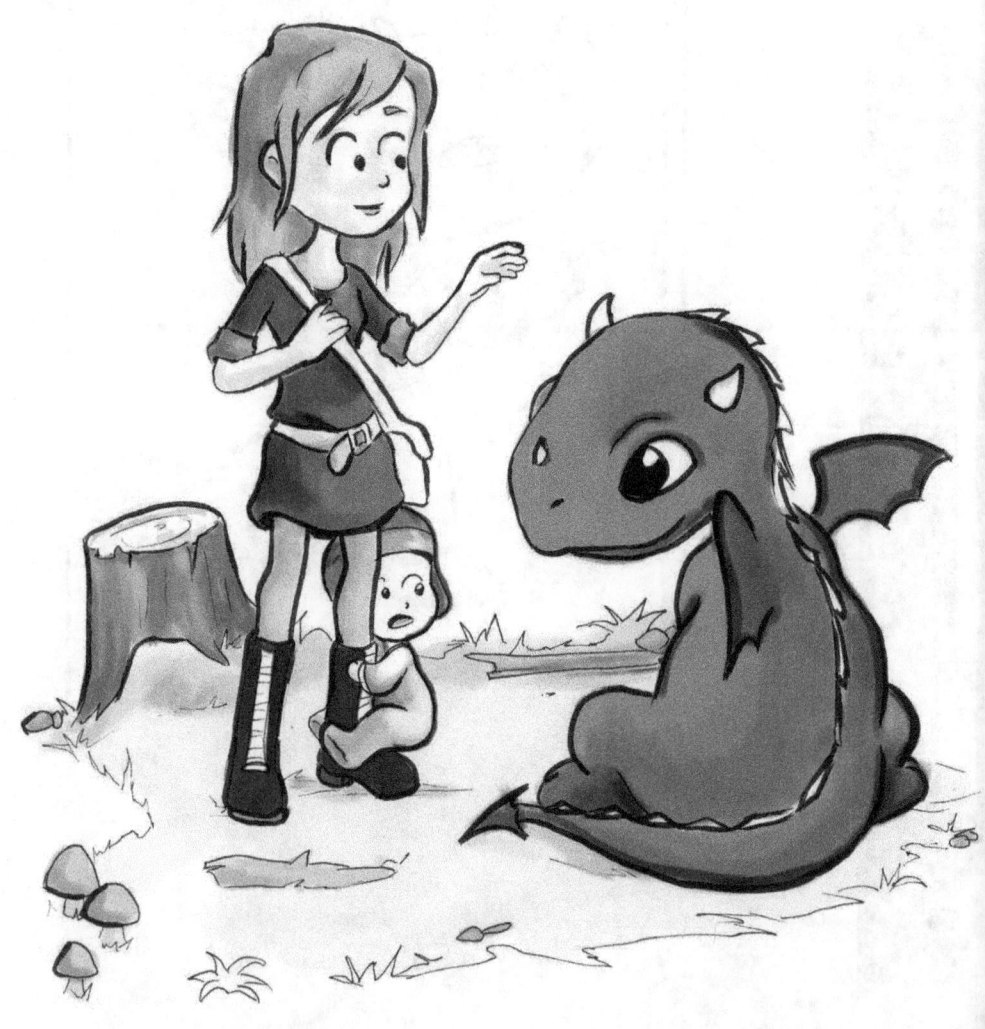

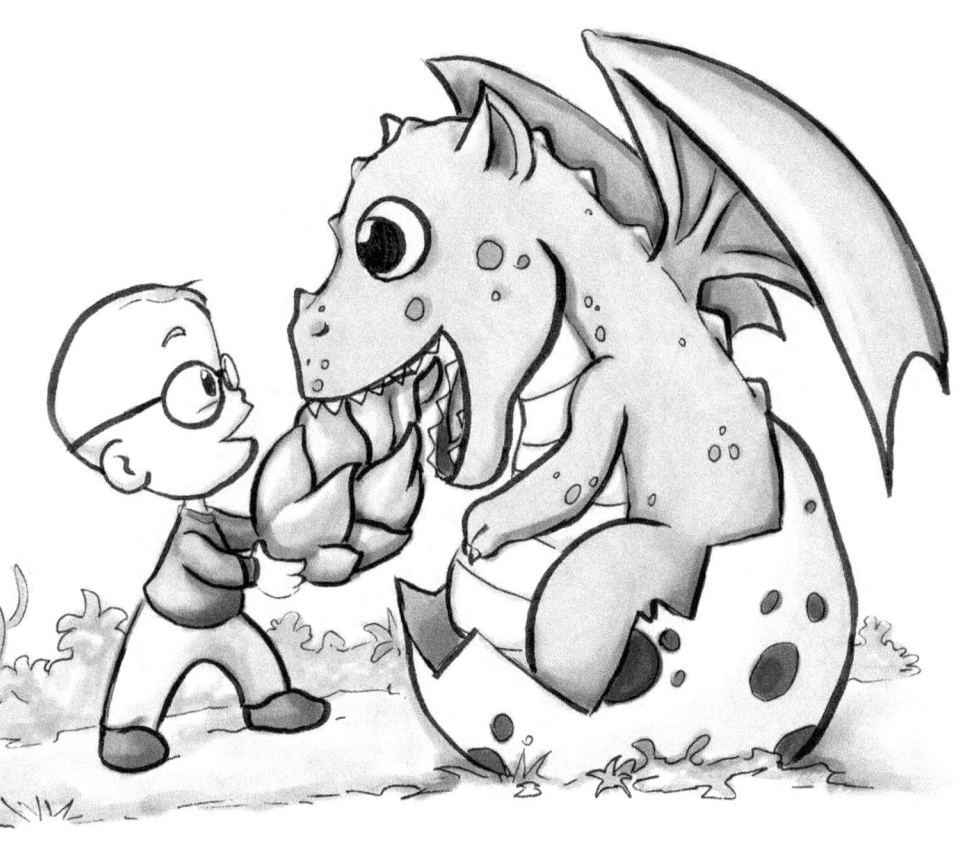

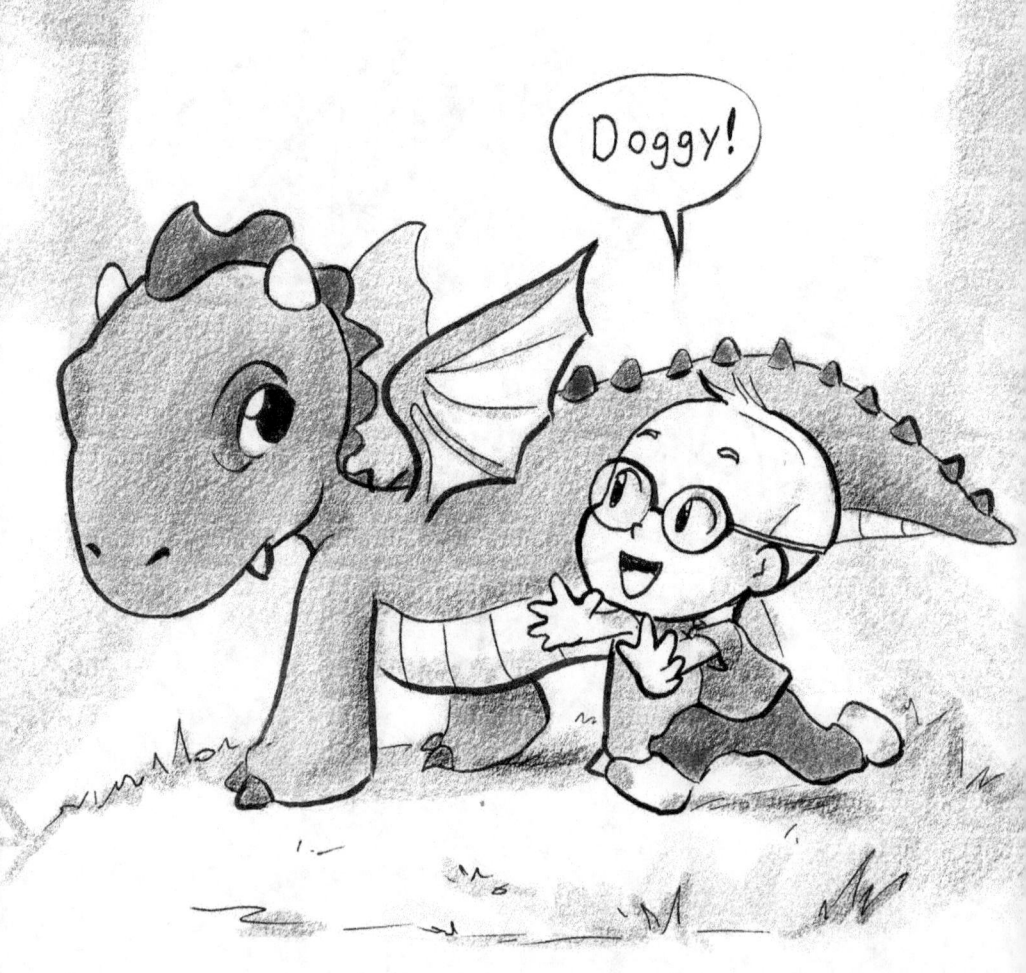

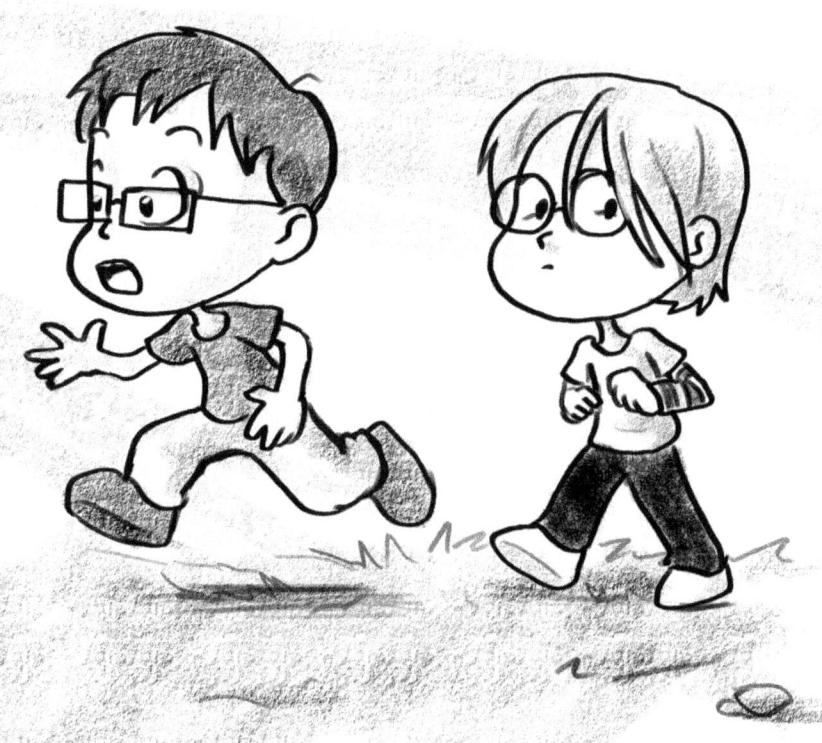

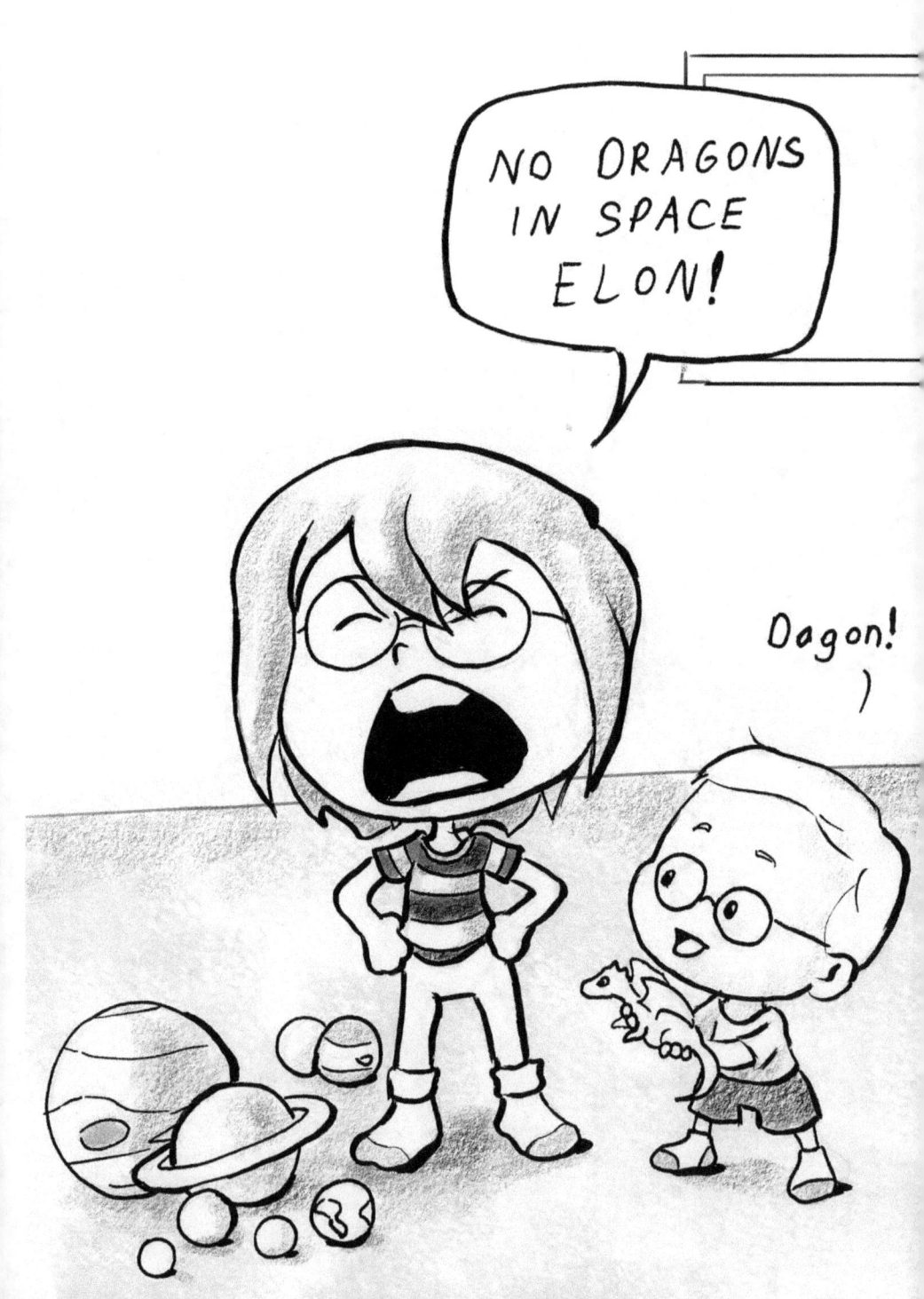

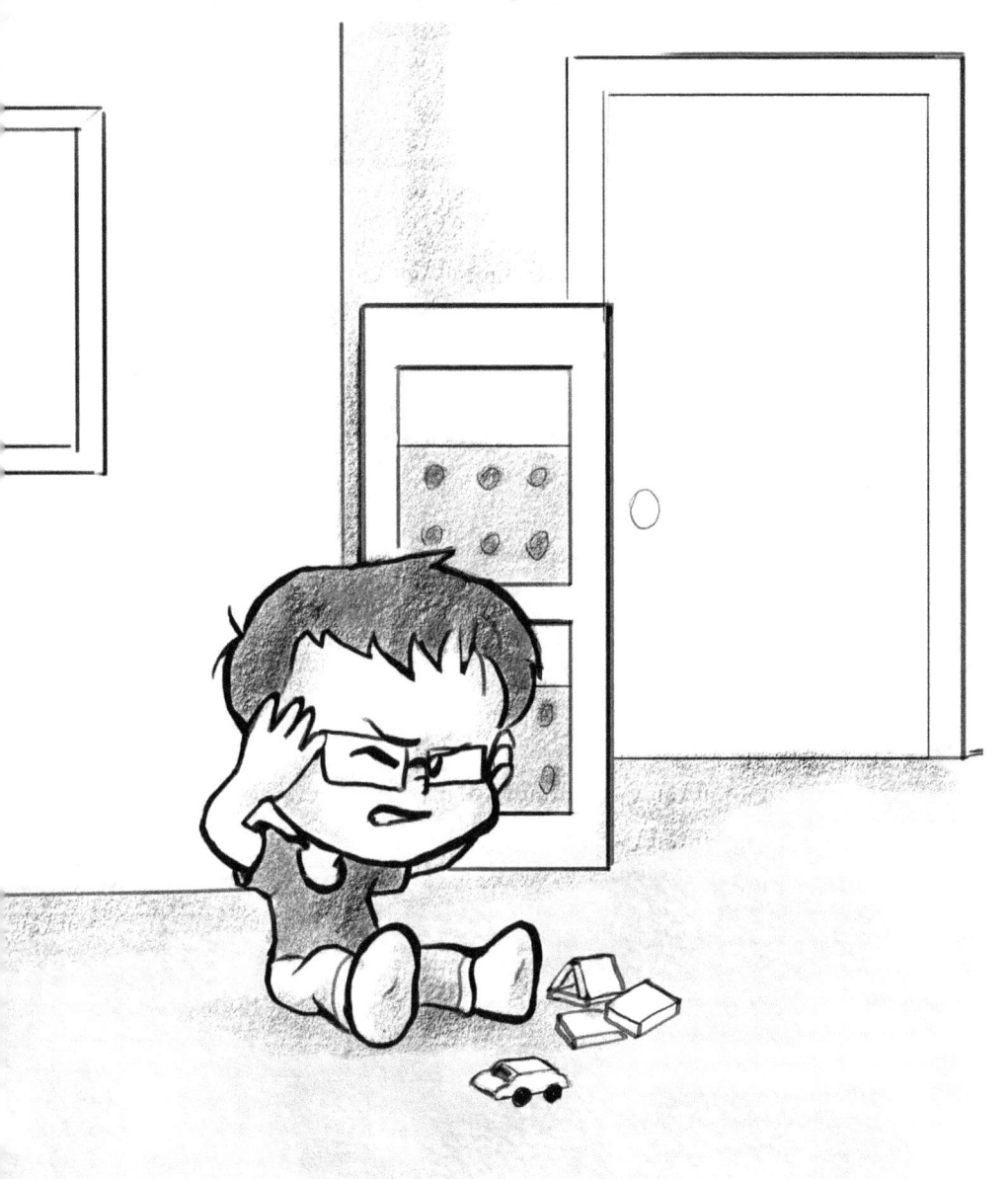

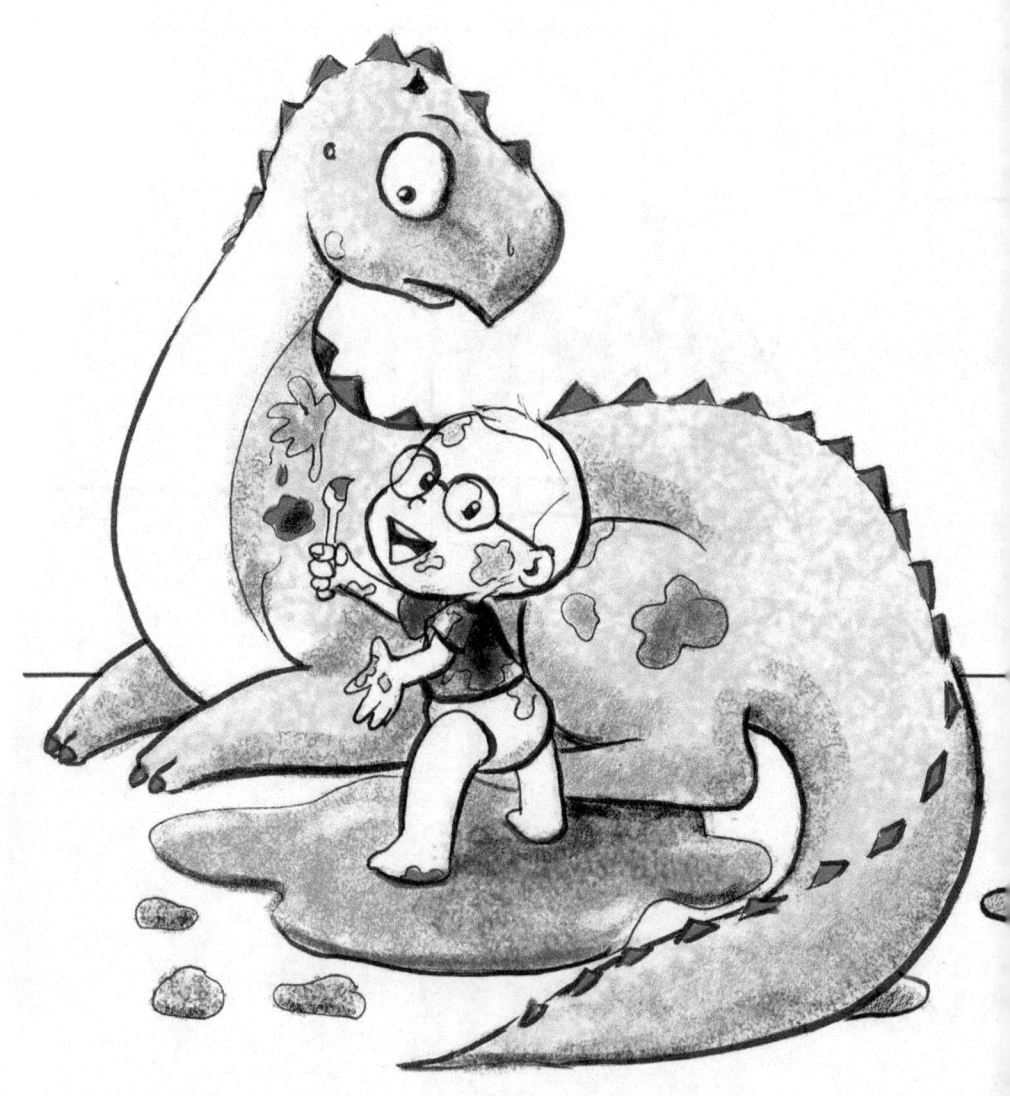

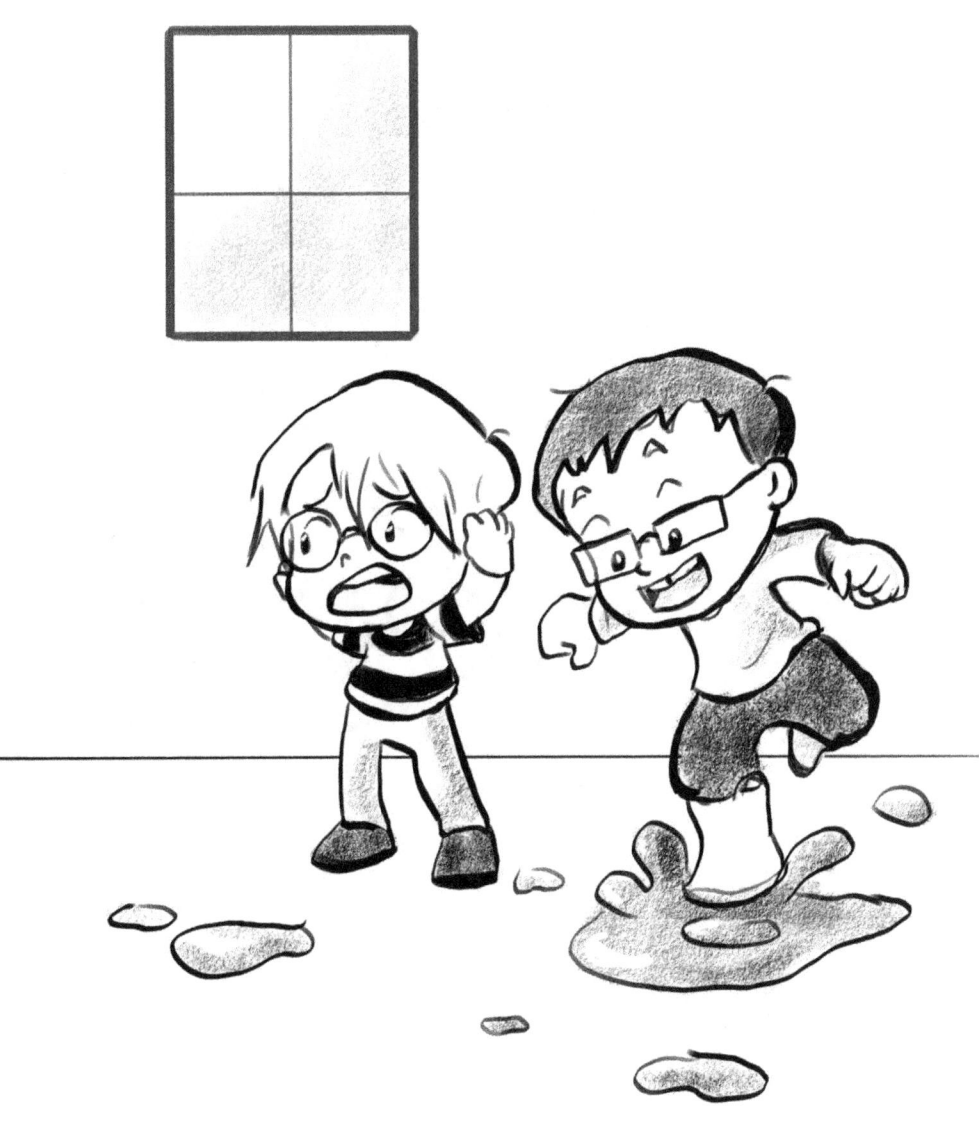

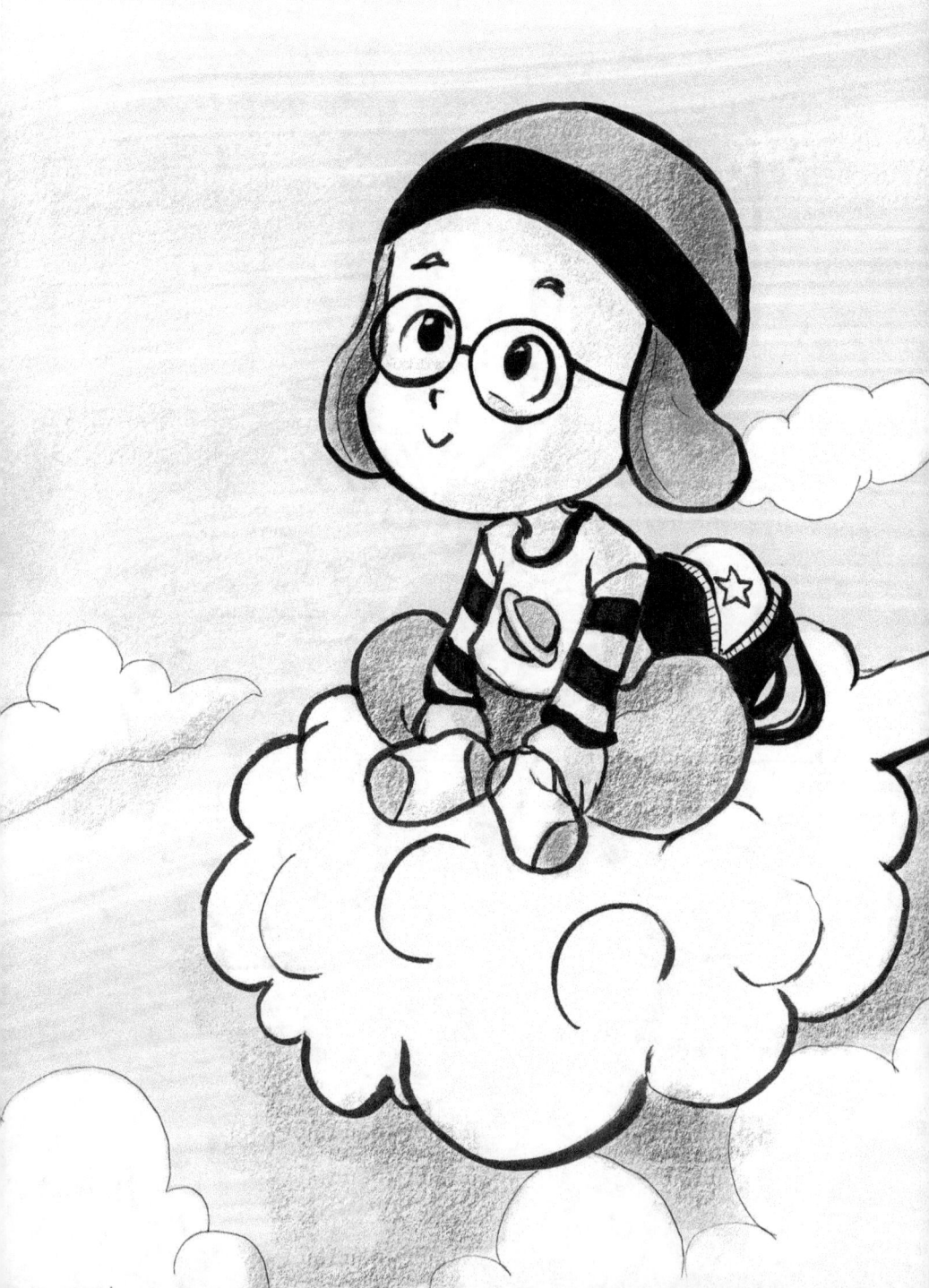

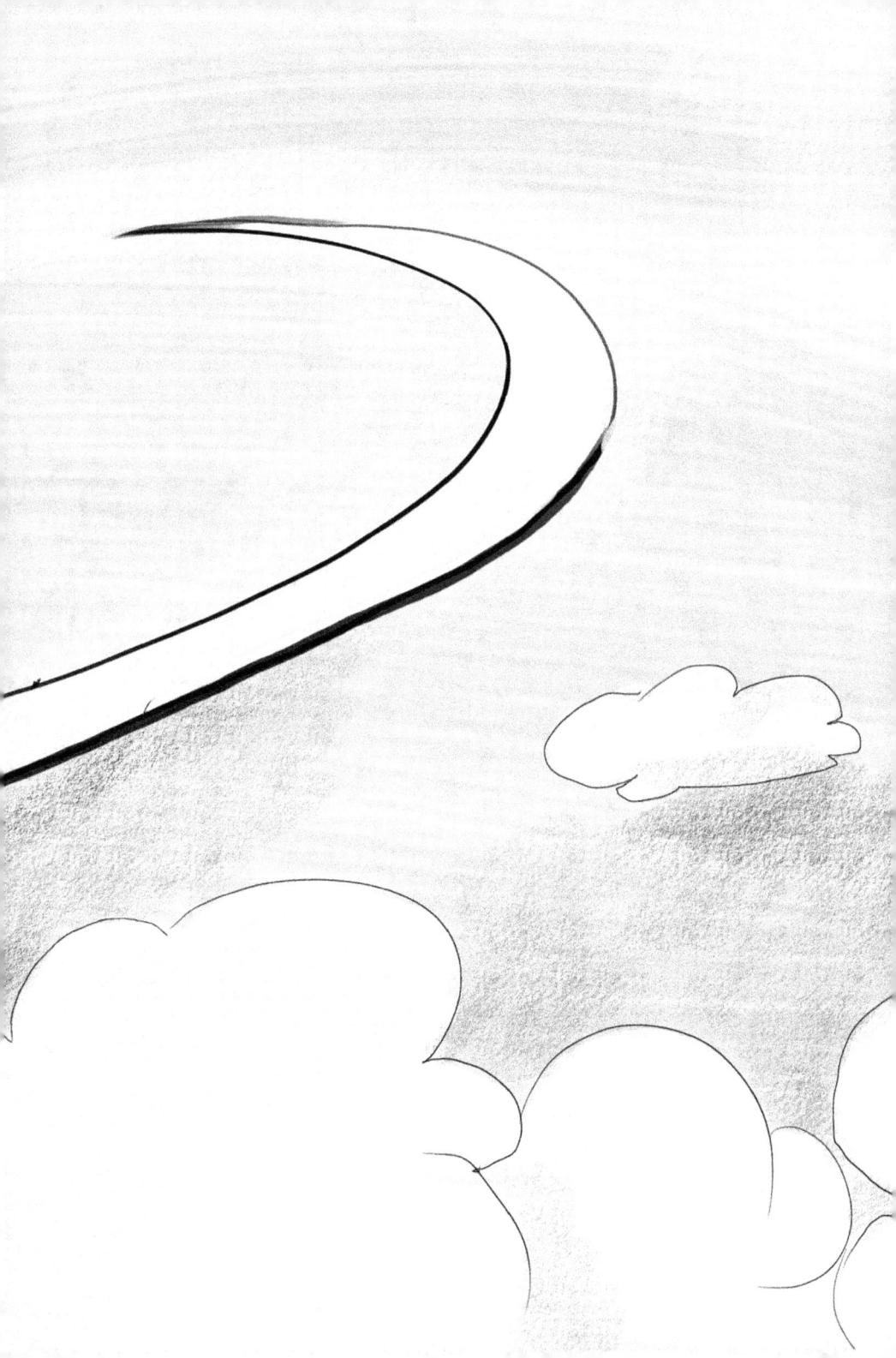

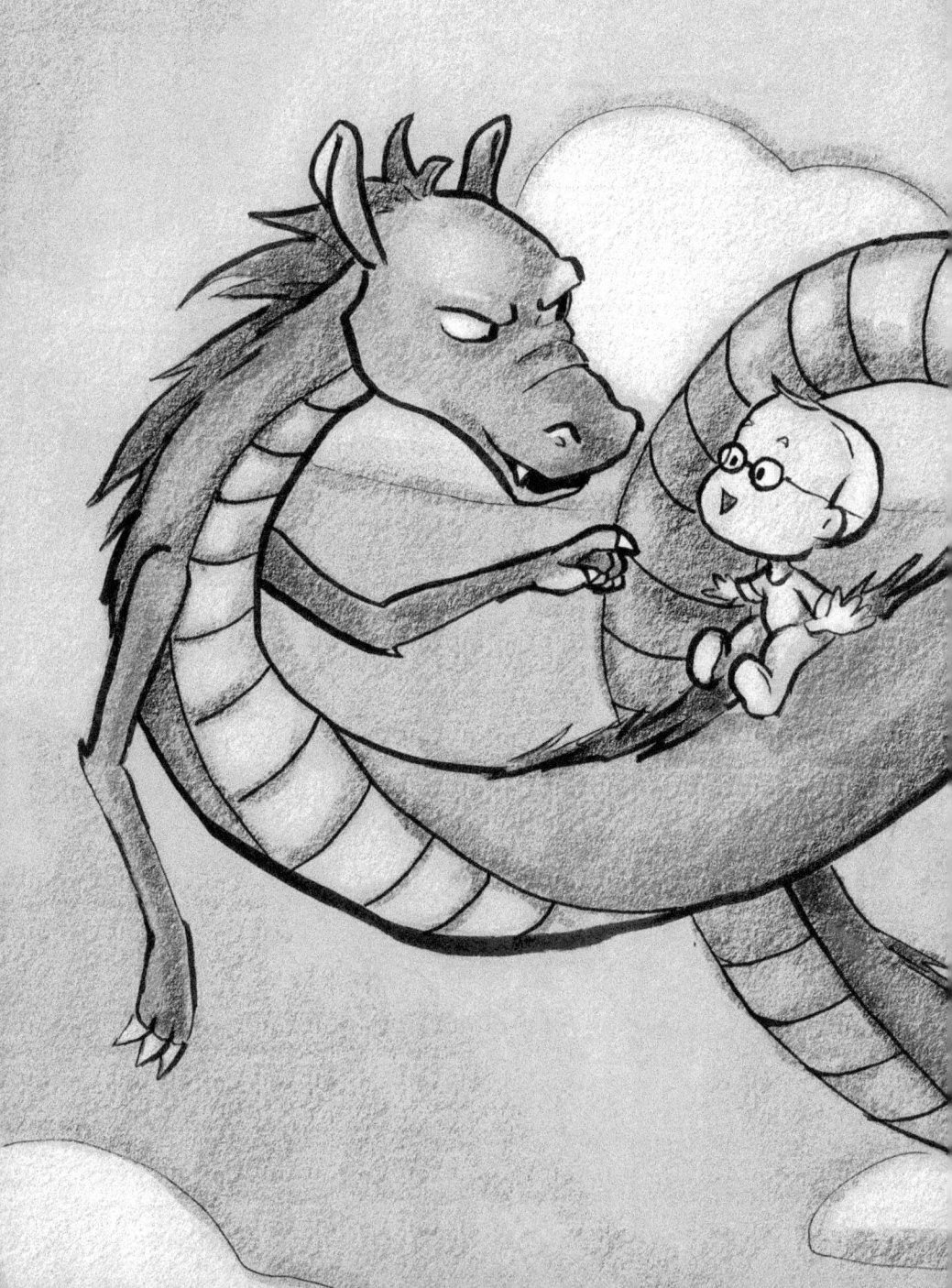

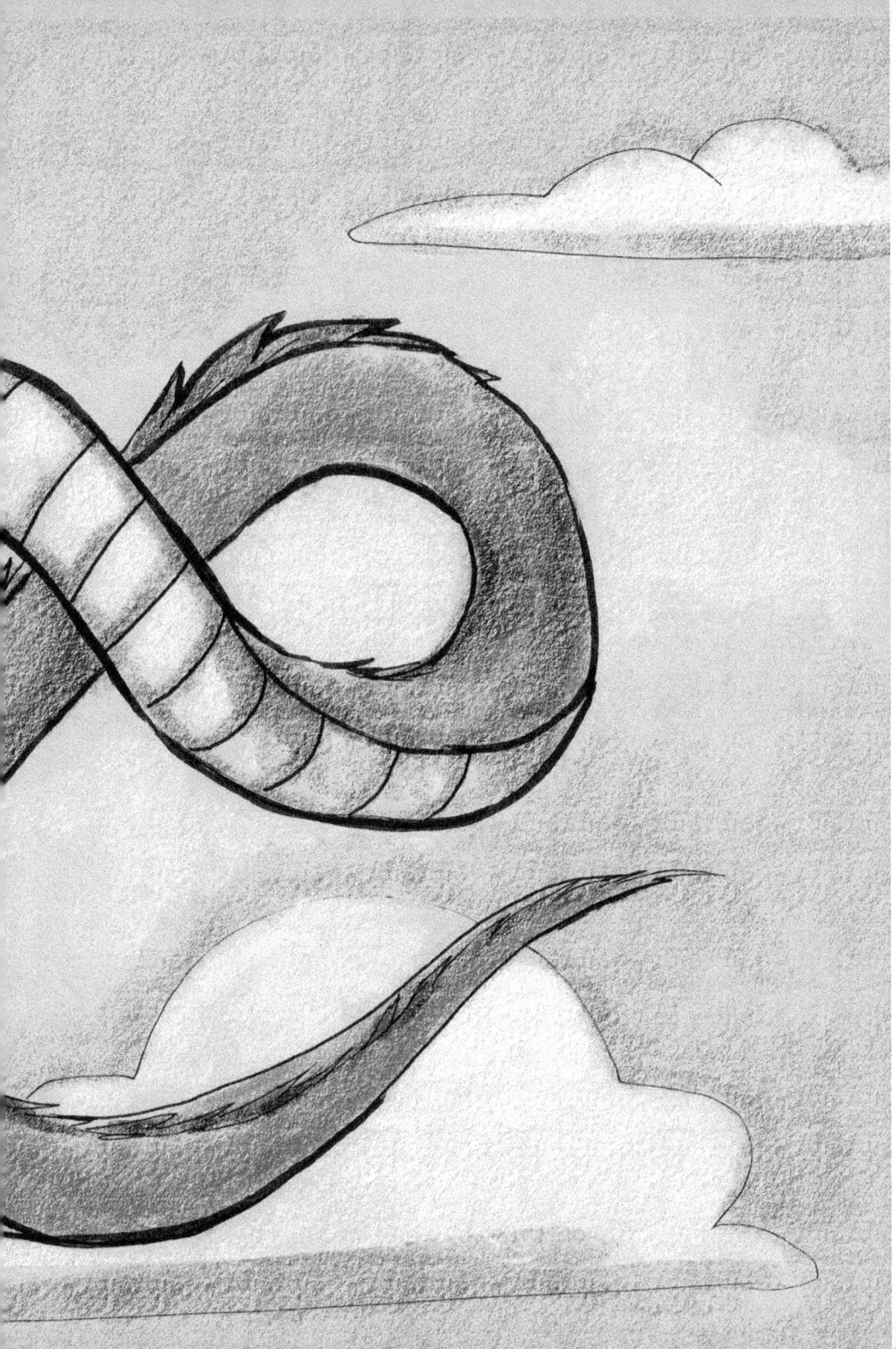

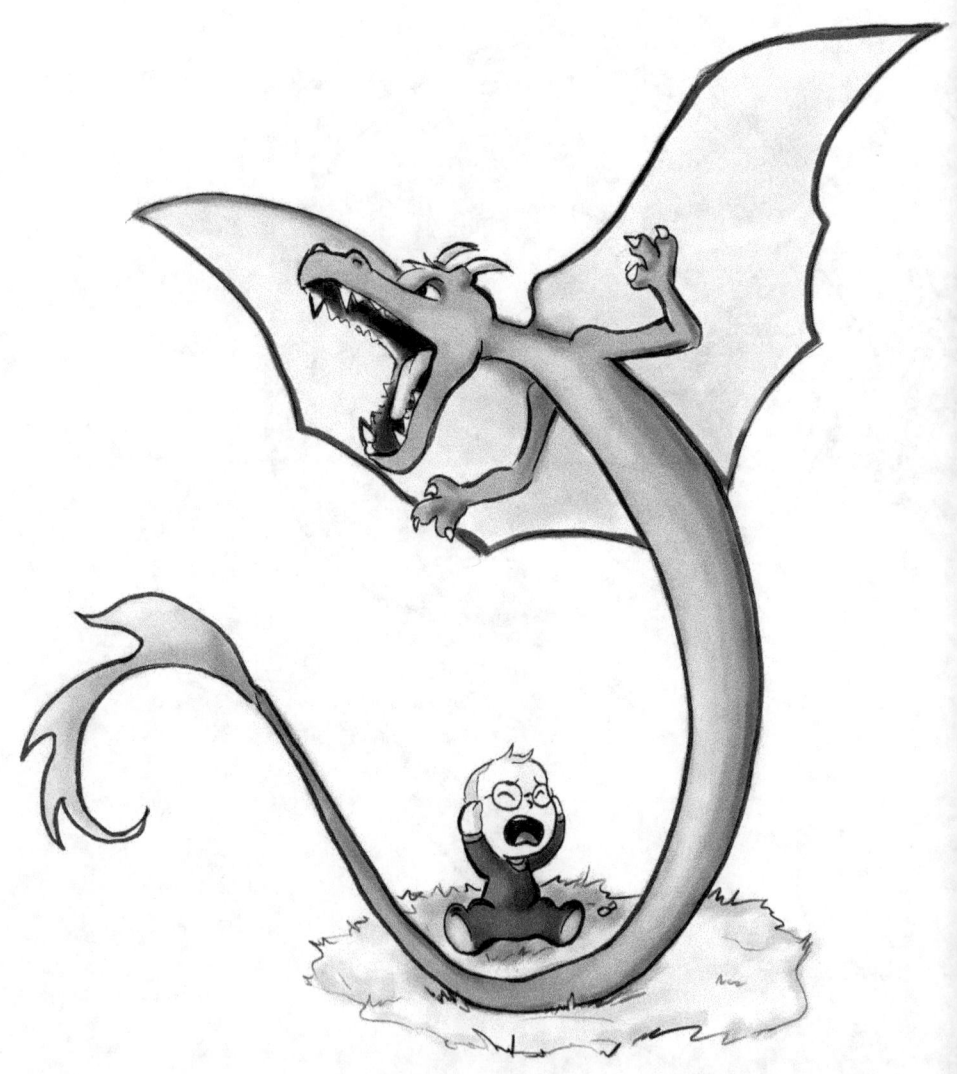

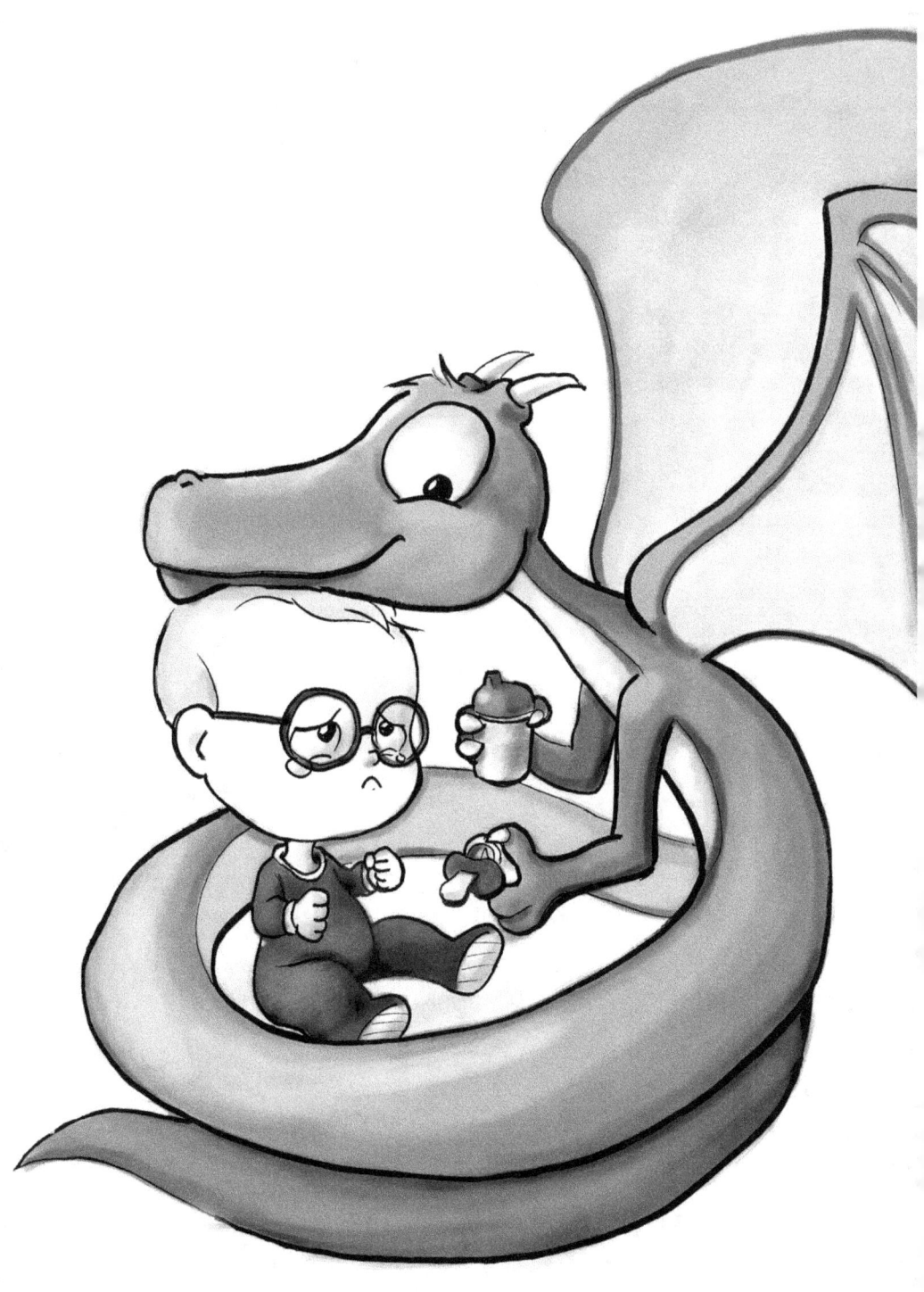

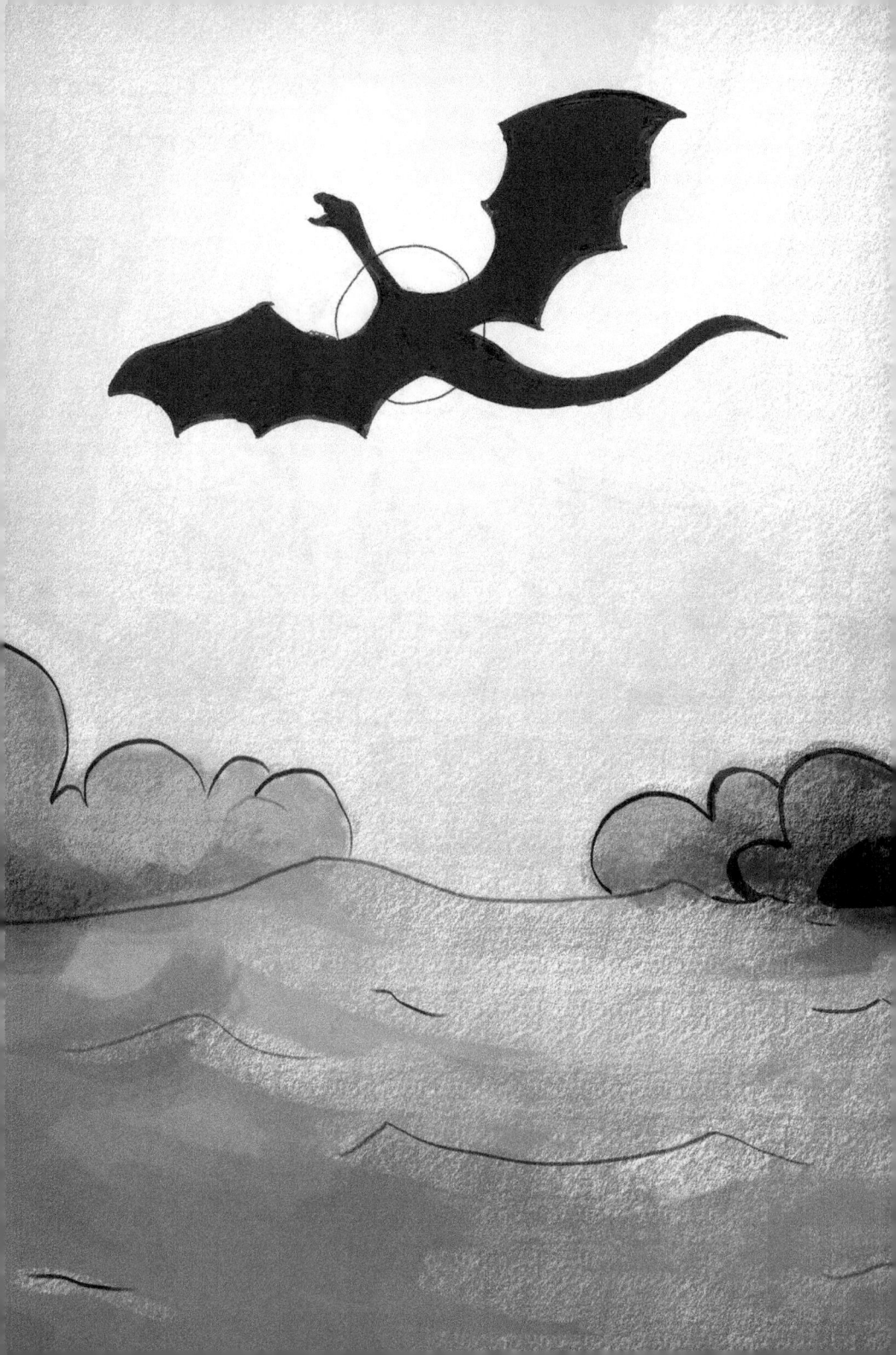

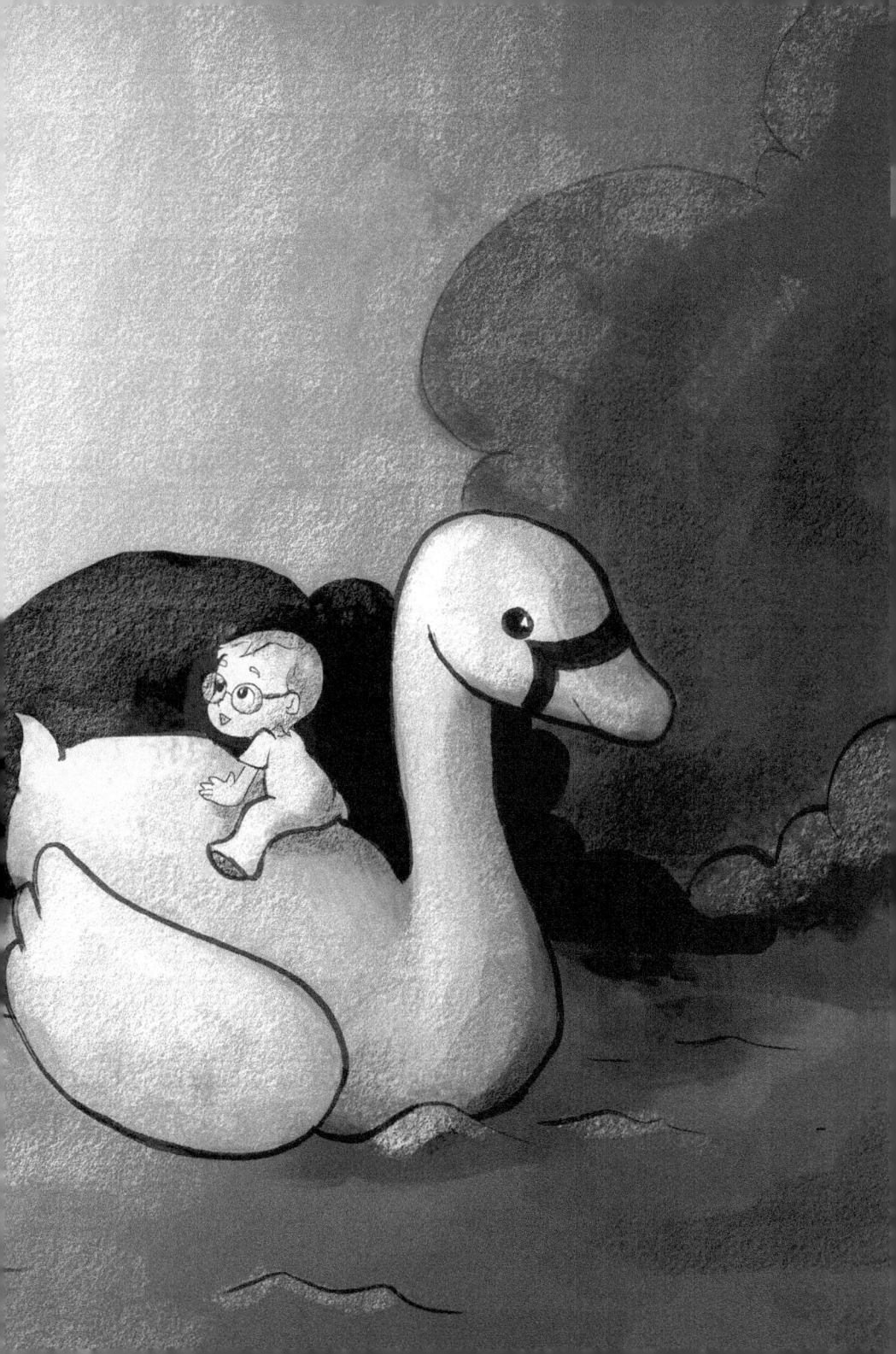

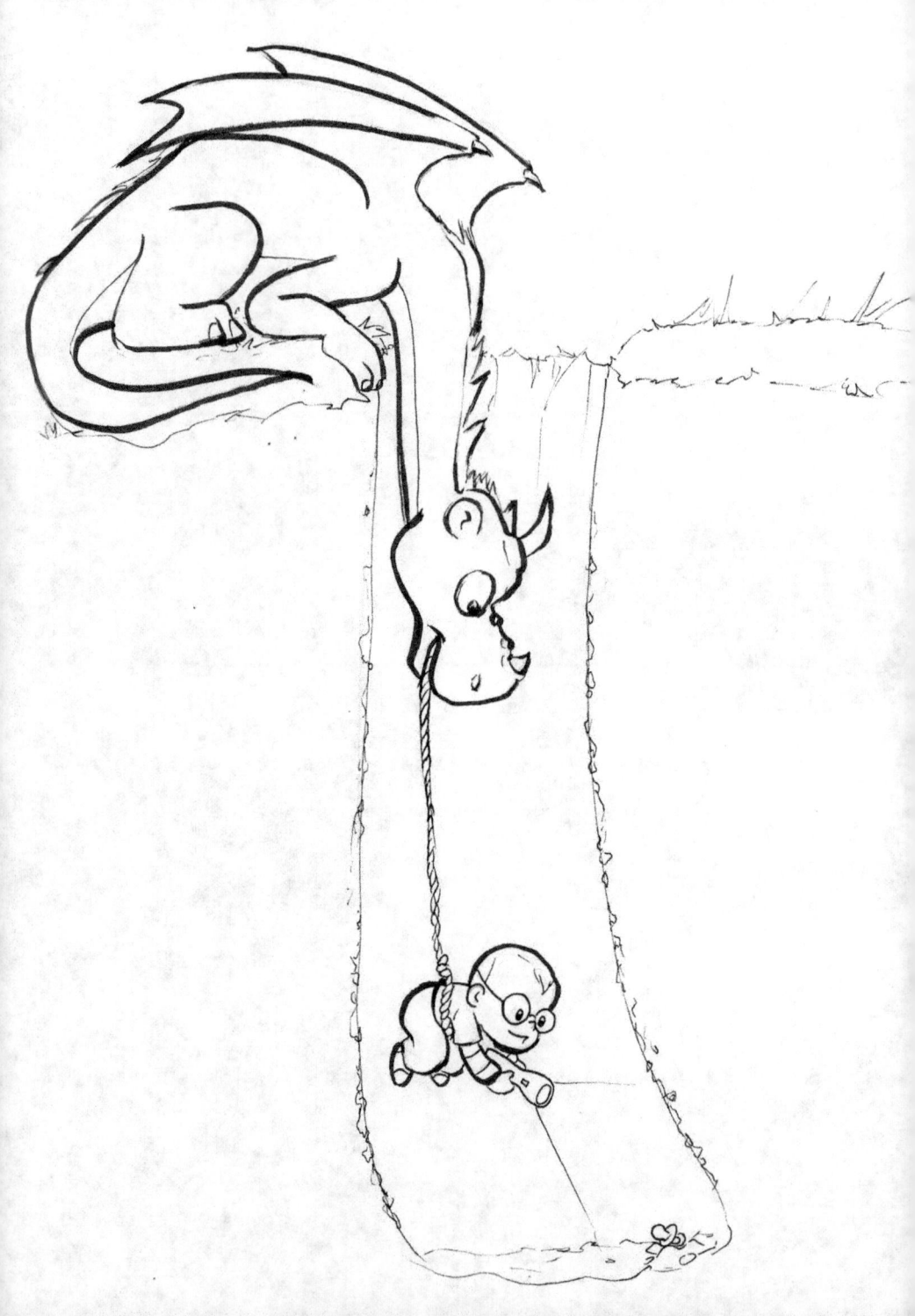

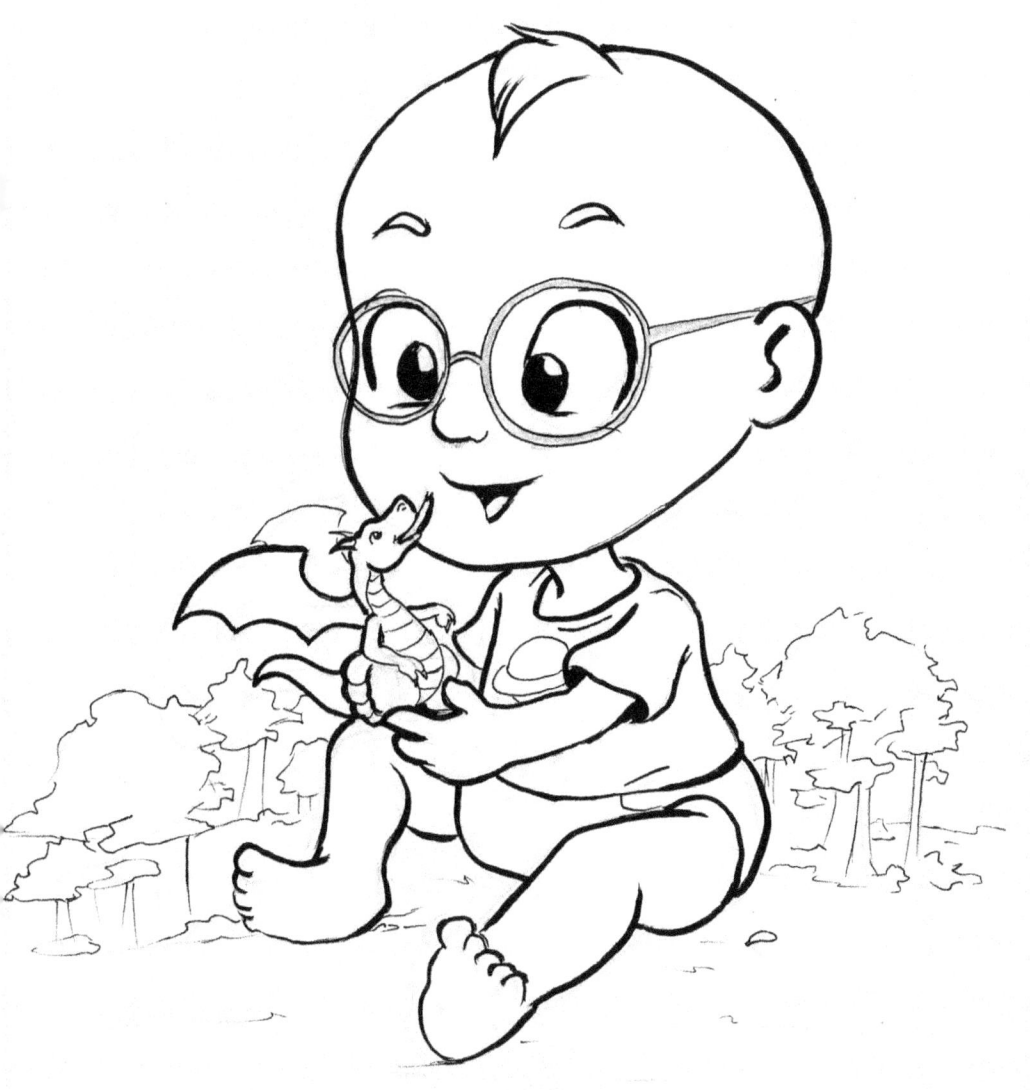

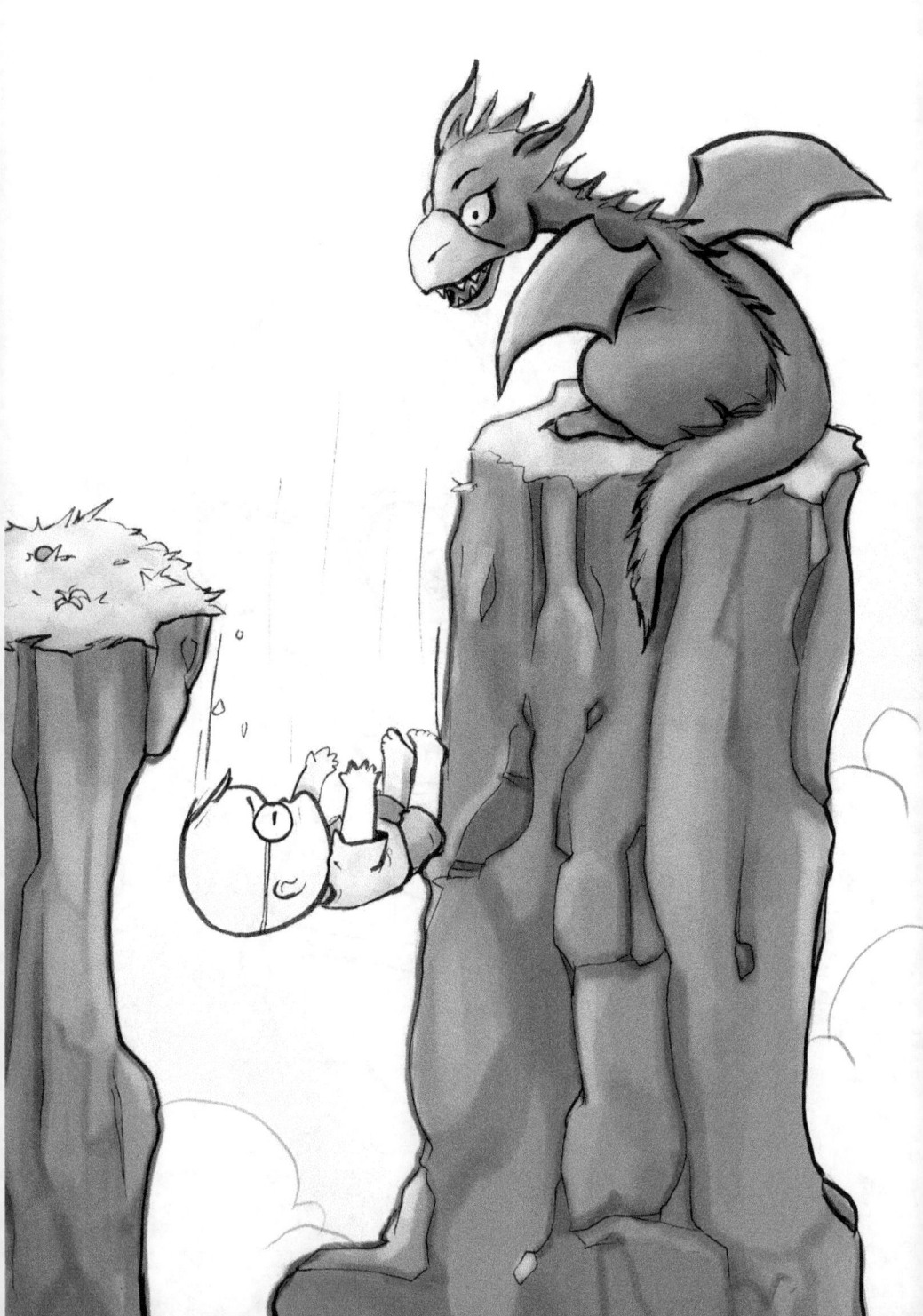

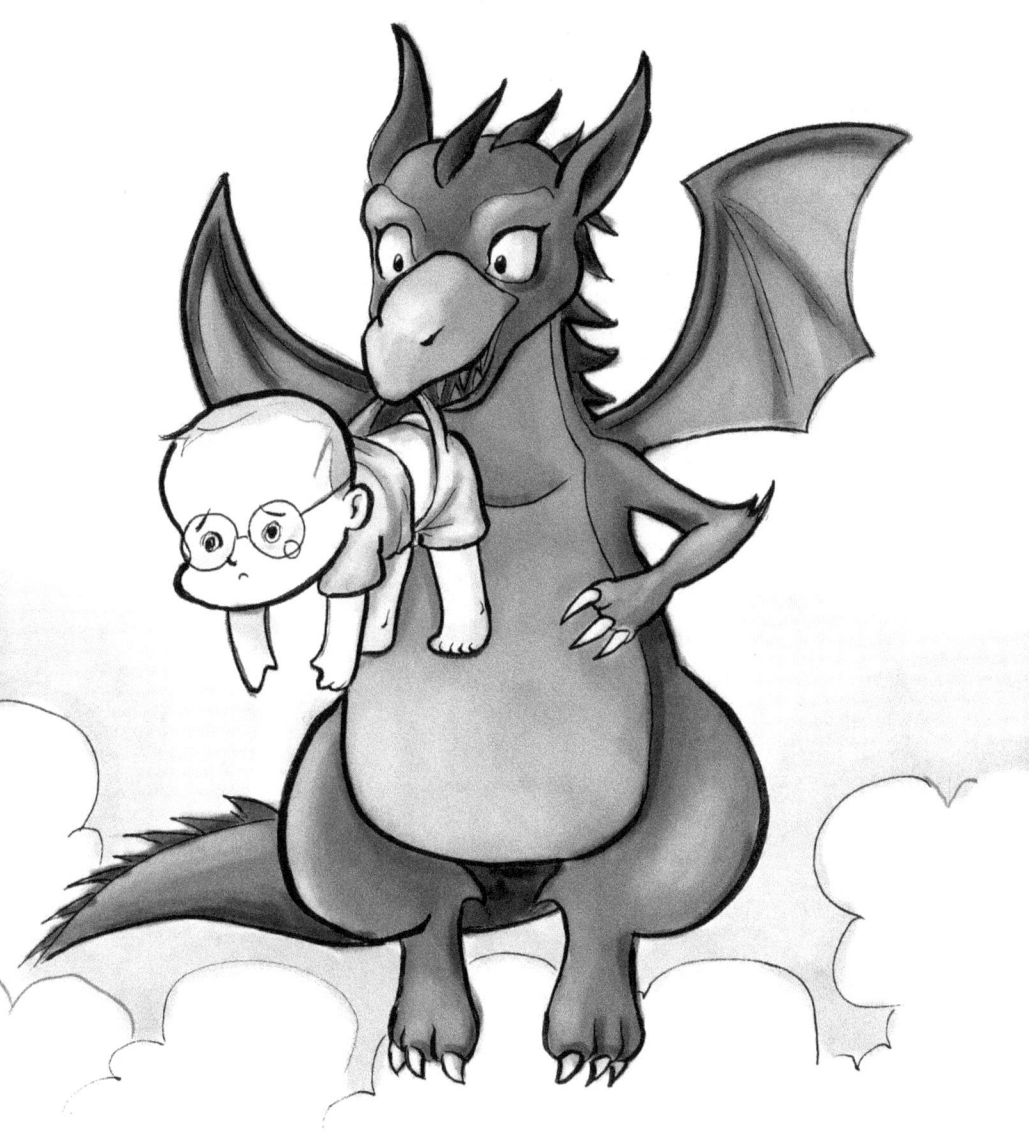

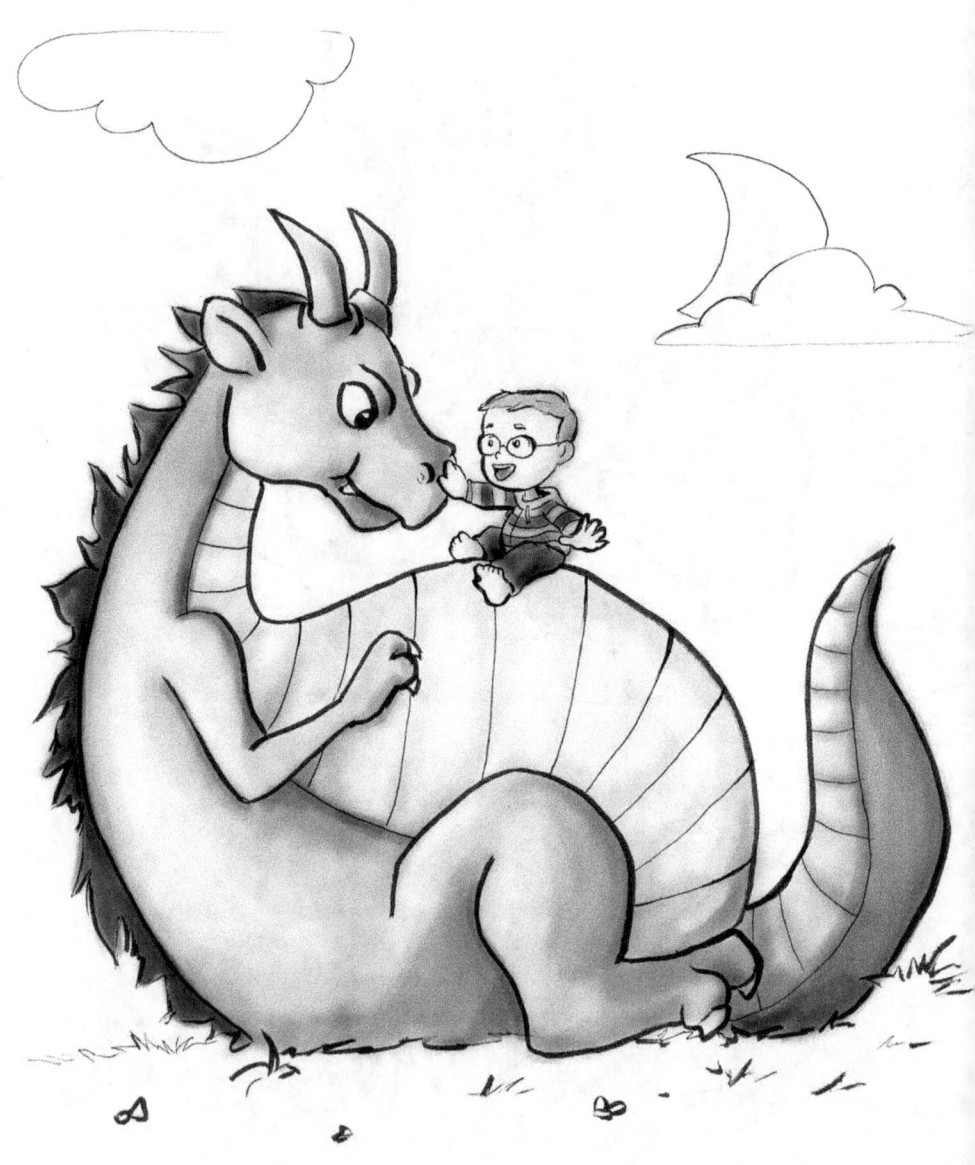

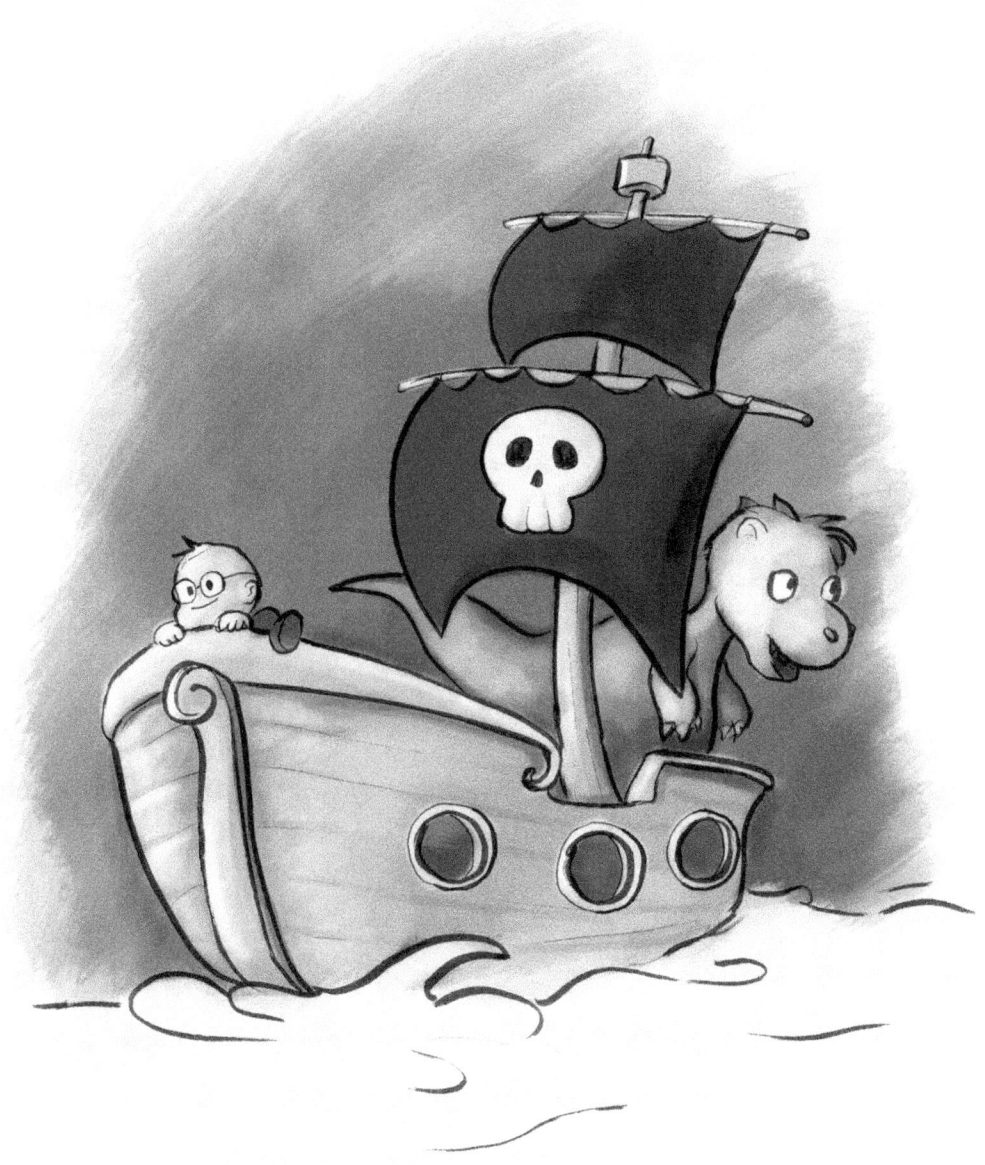

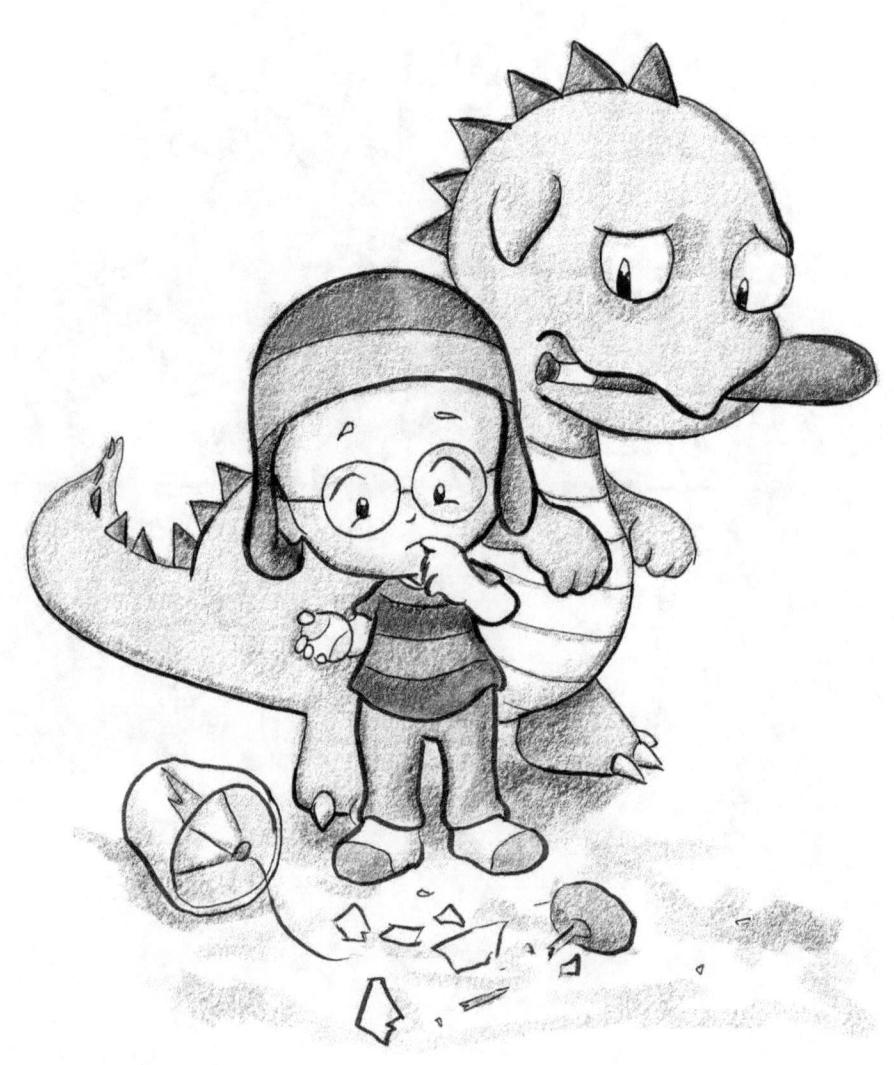

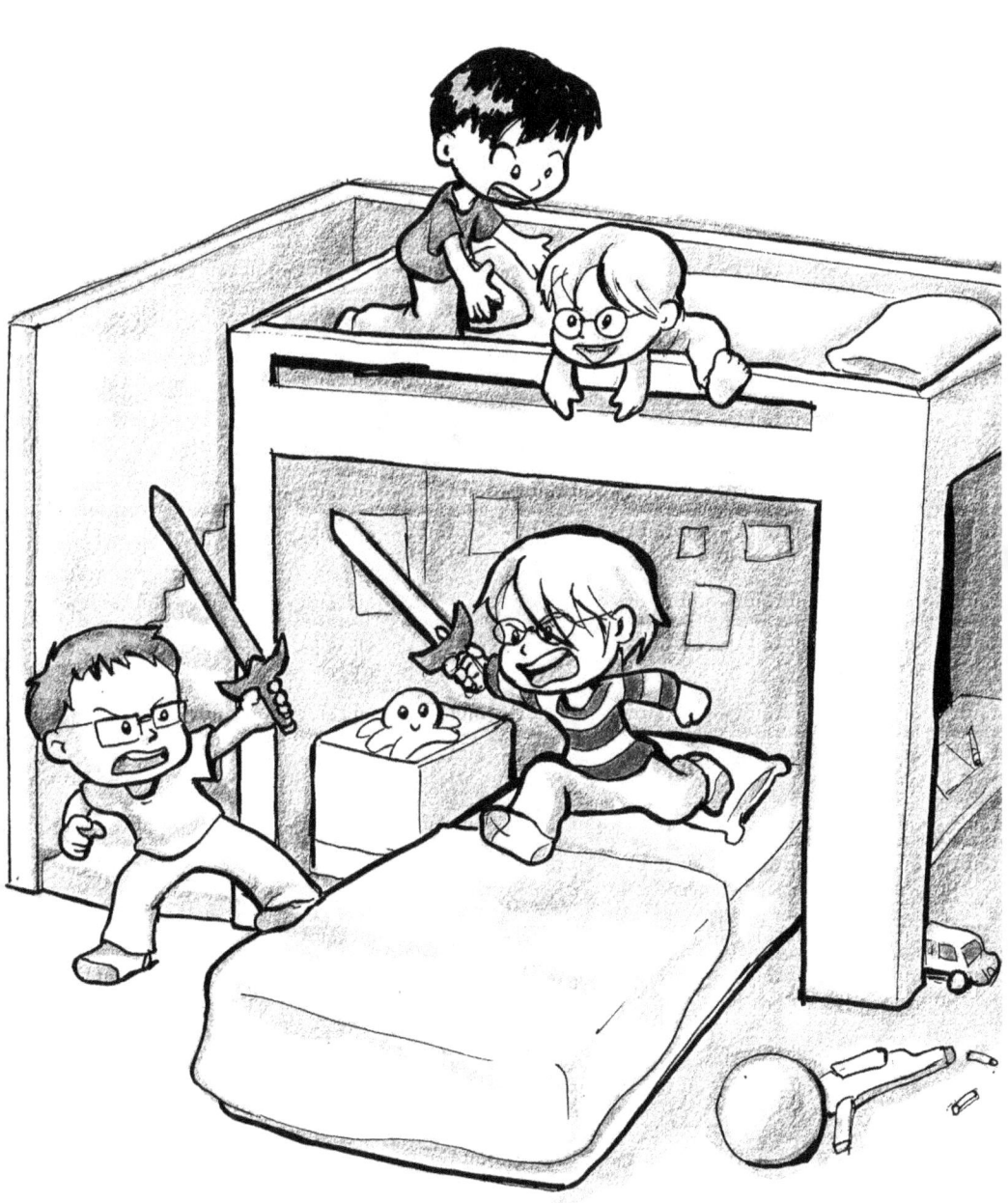

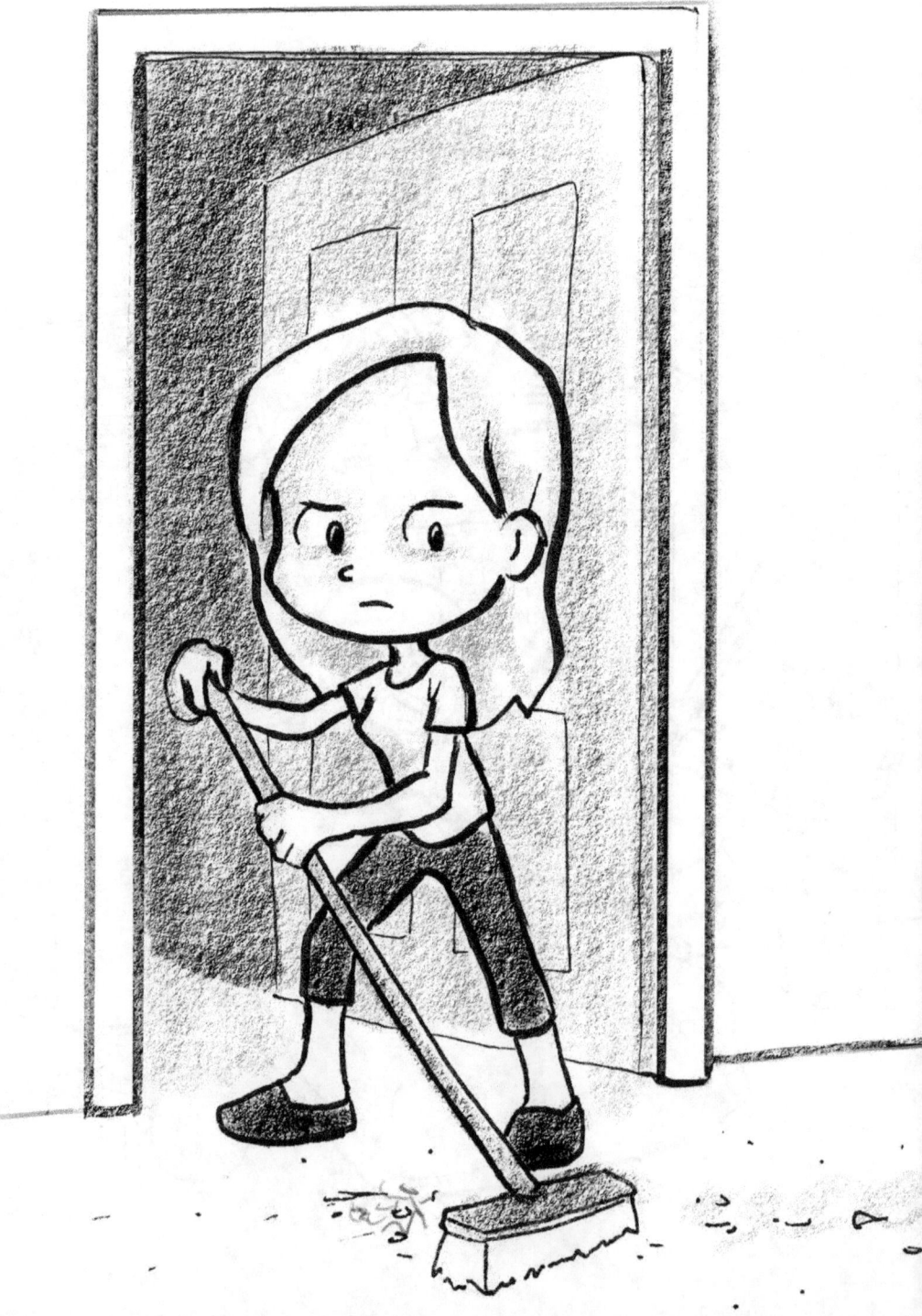

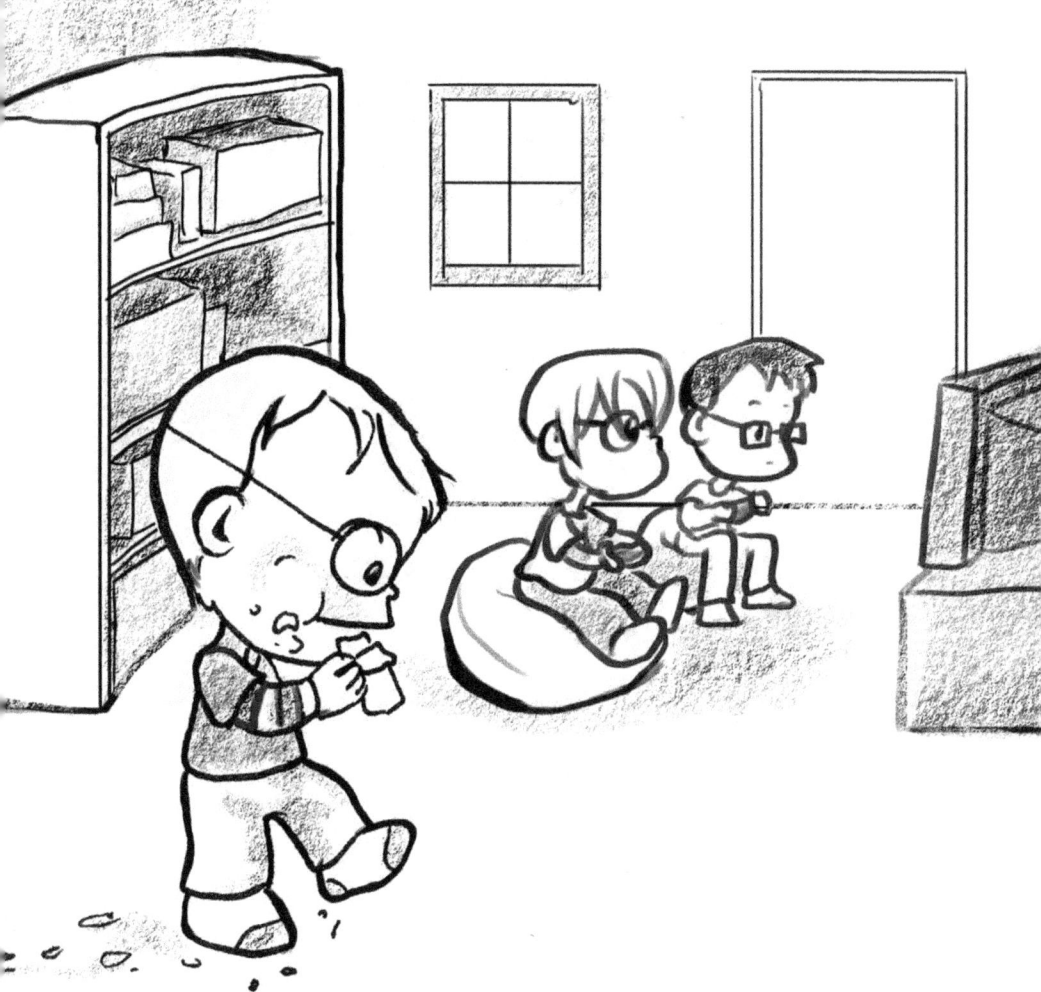

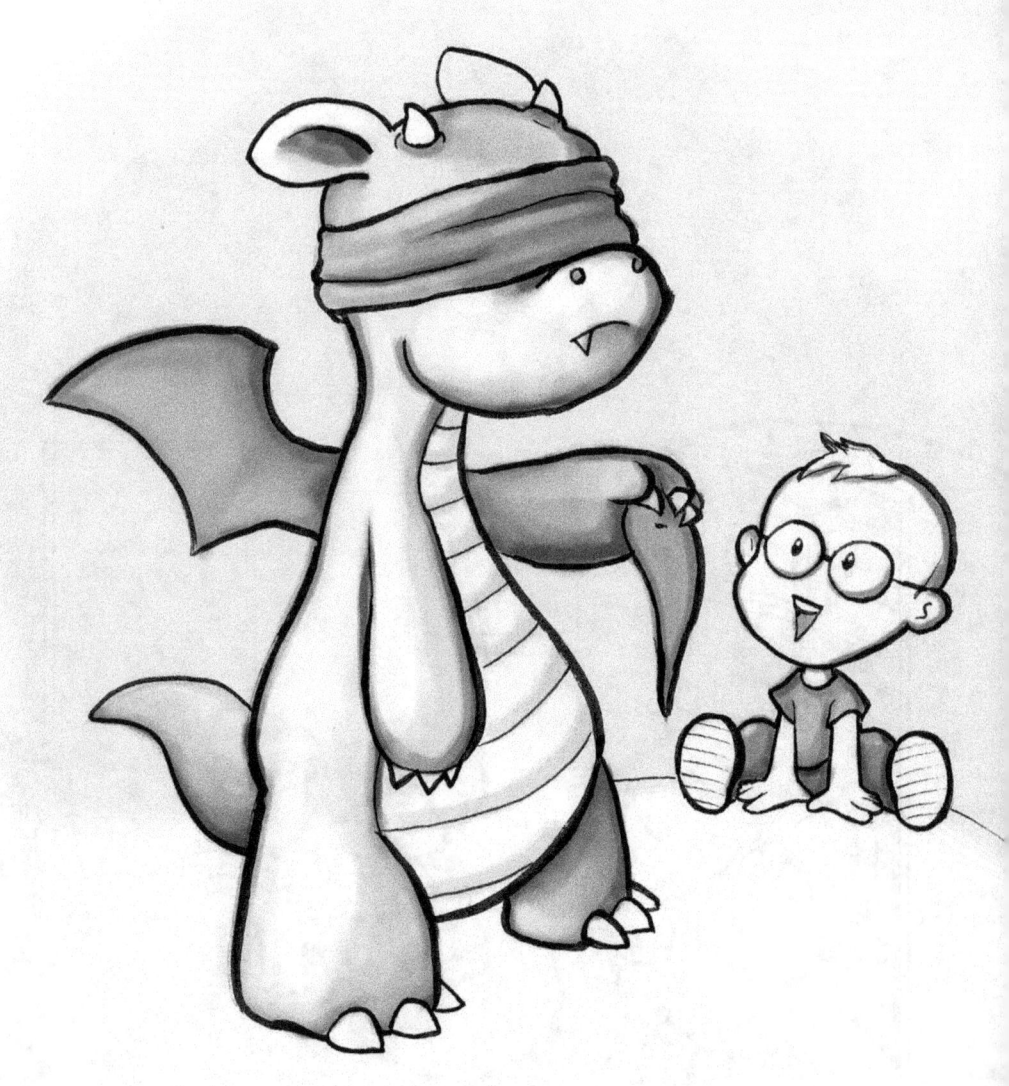

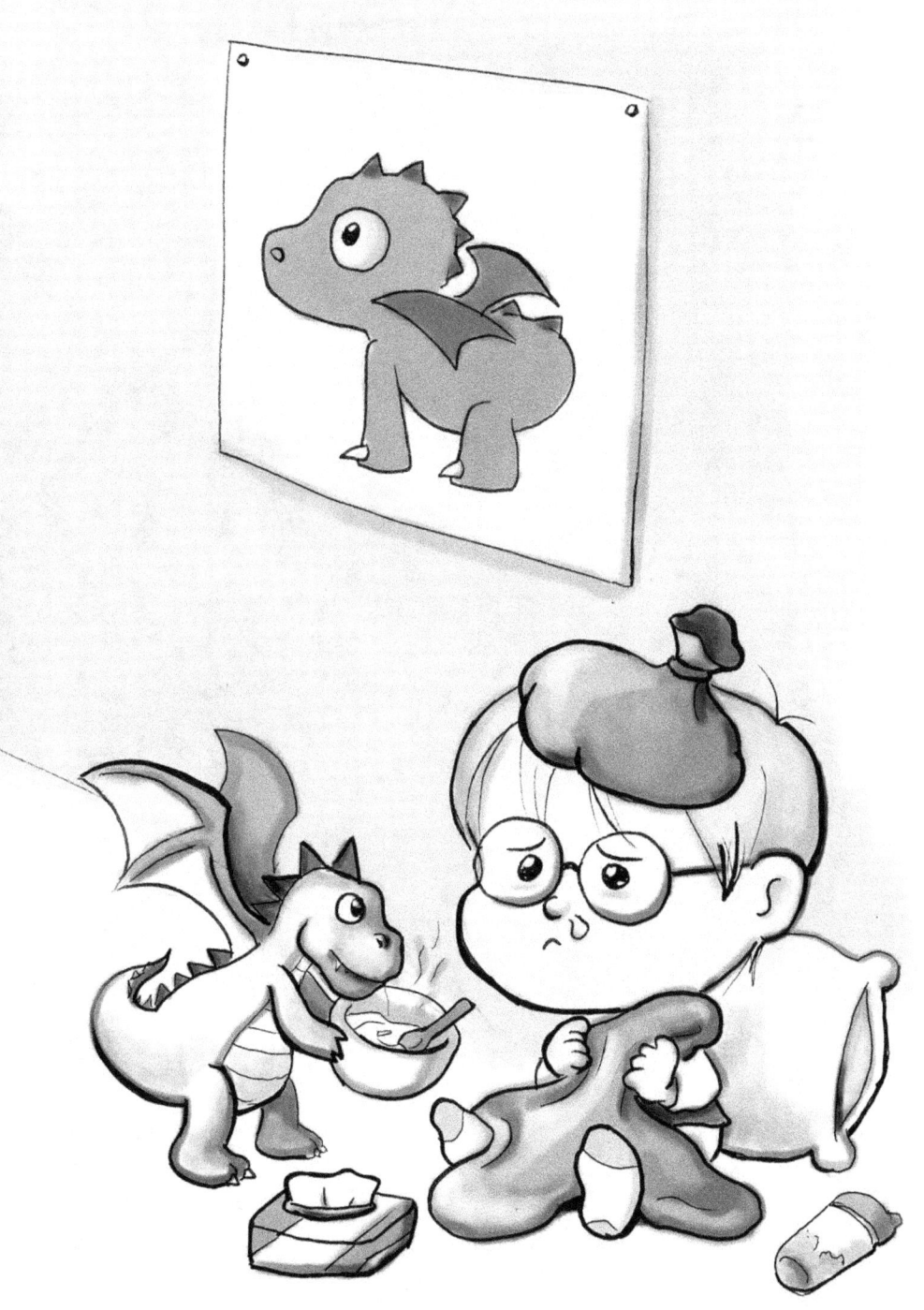

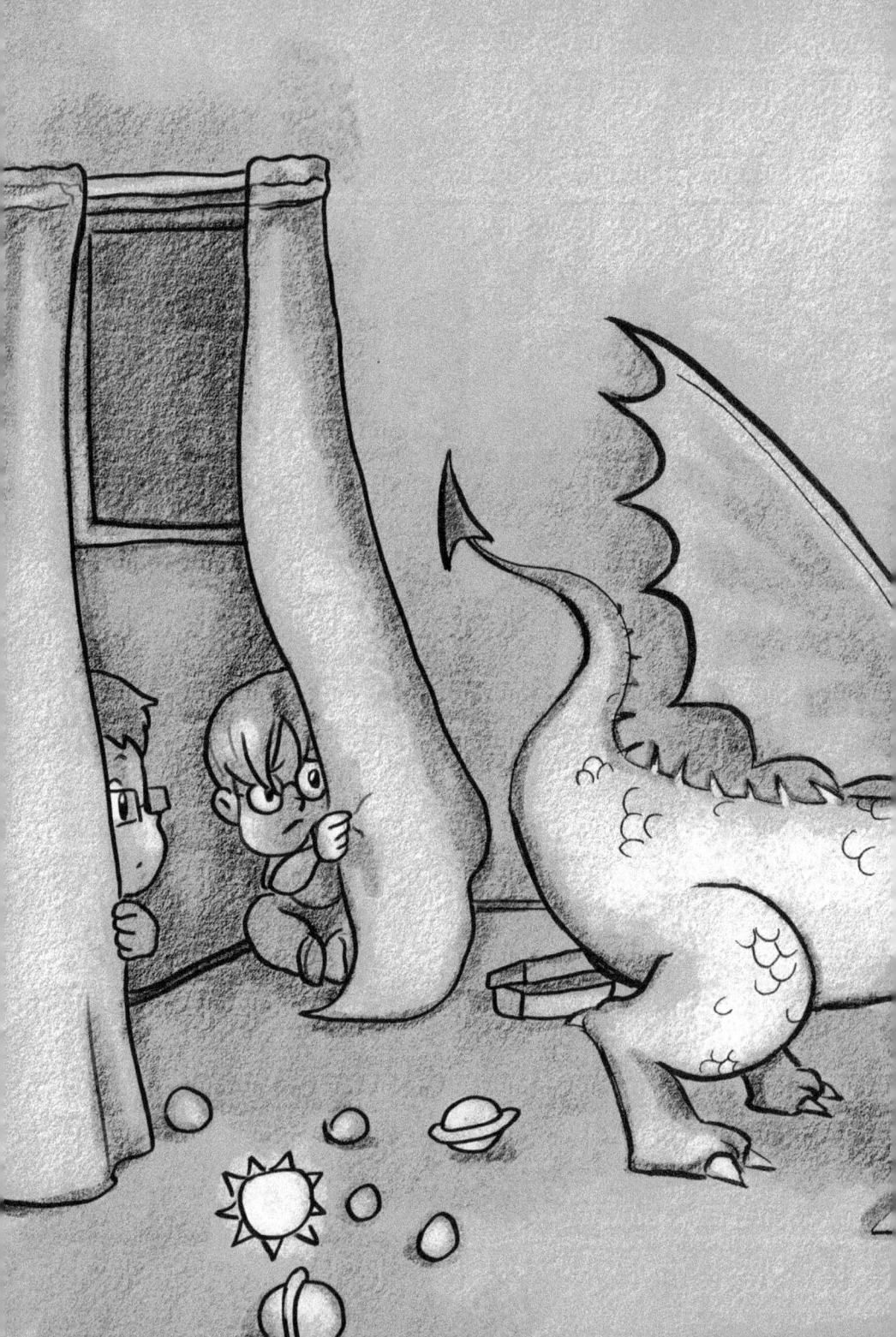

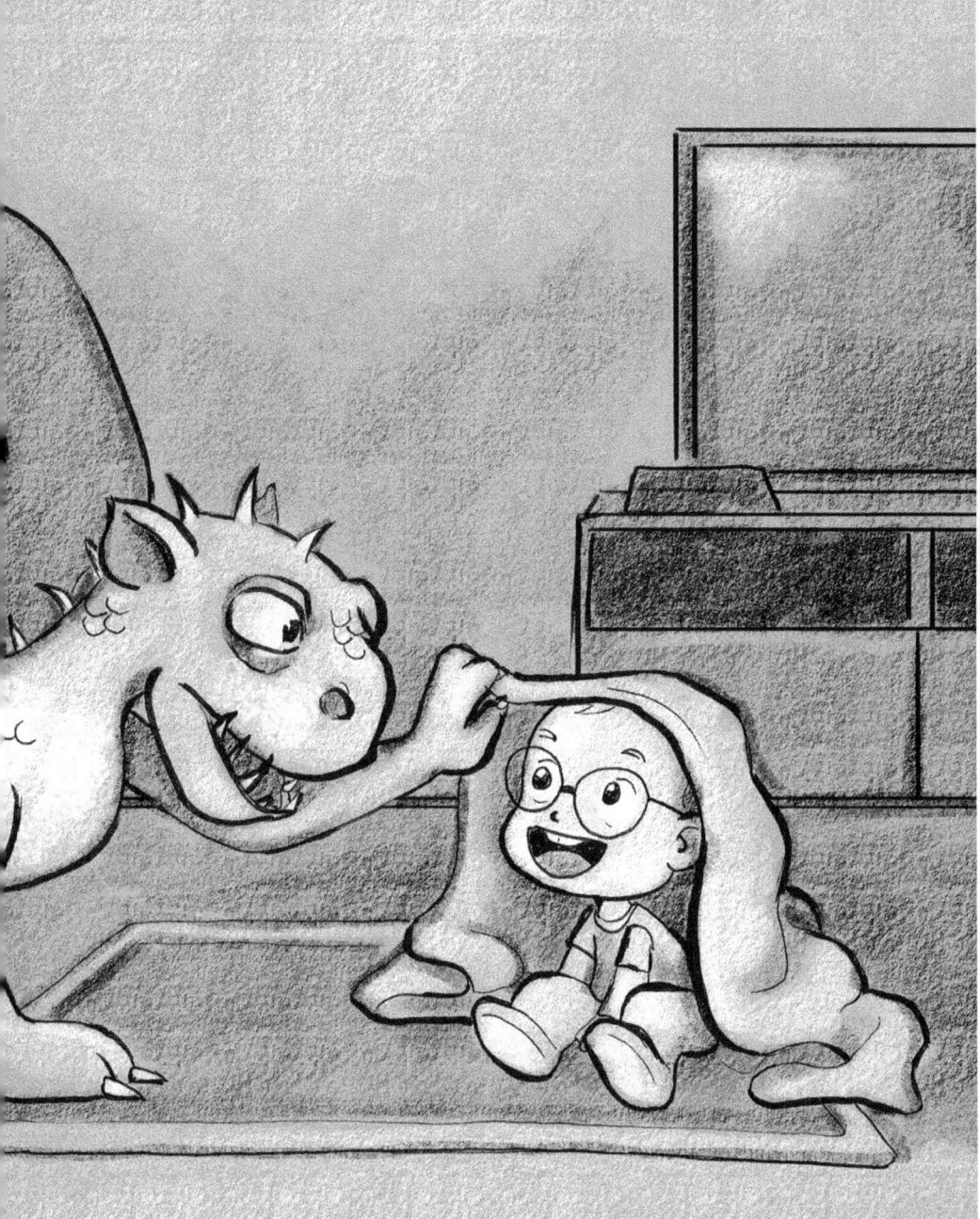

In my home, we have to turn
the sun off at bedtime.

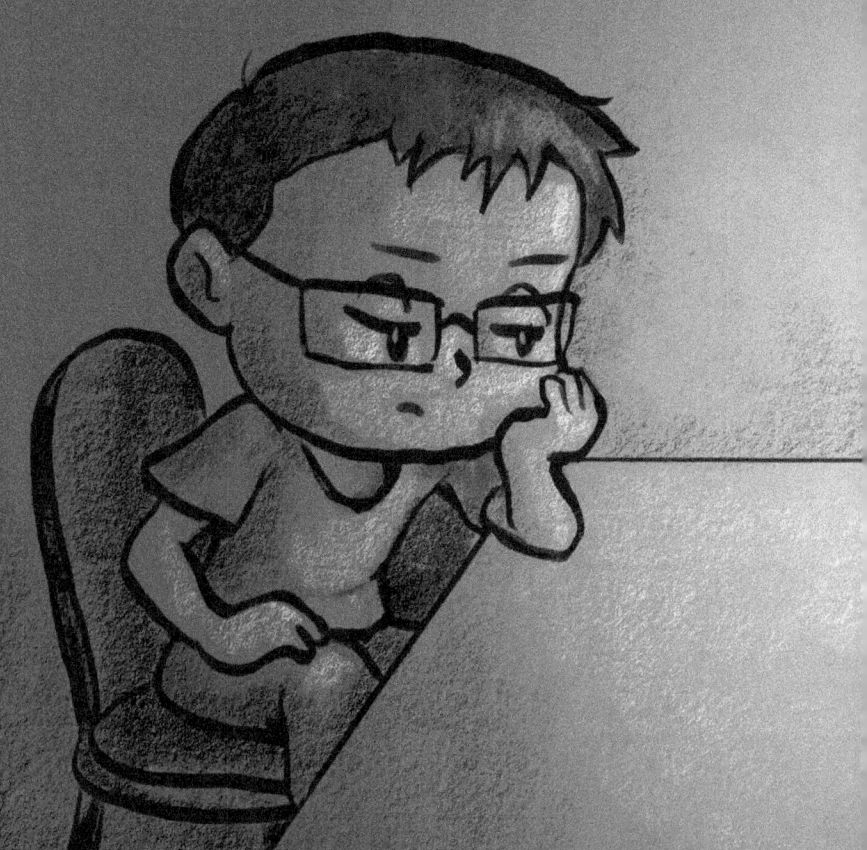

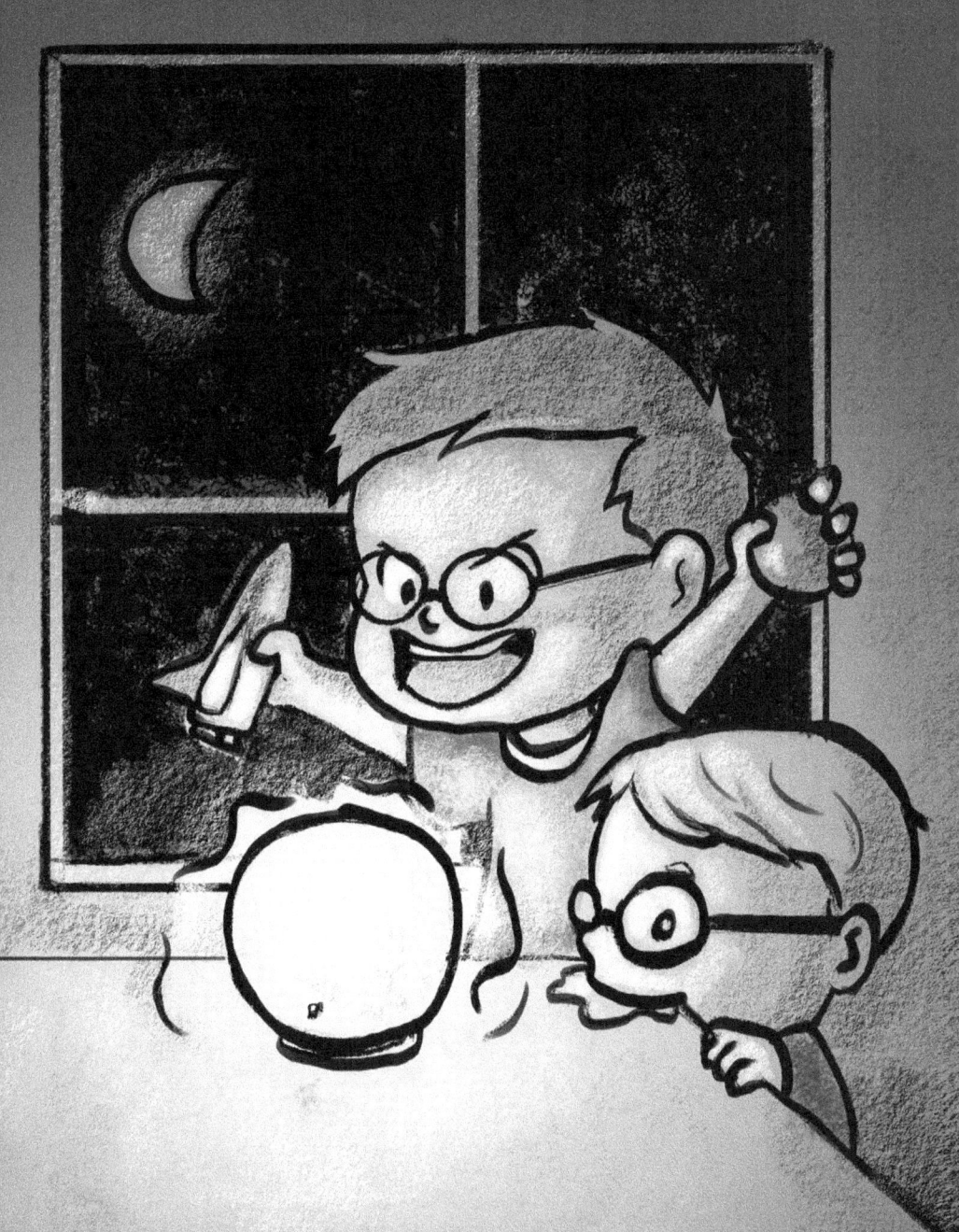

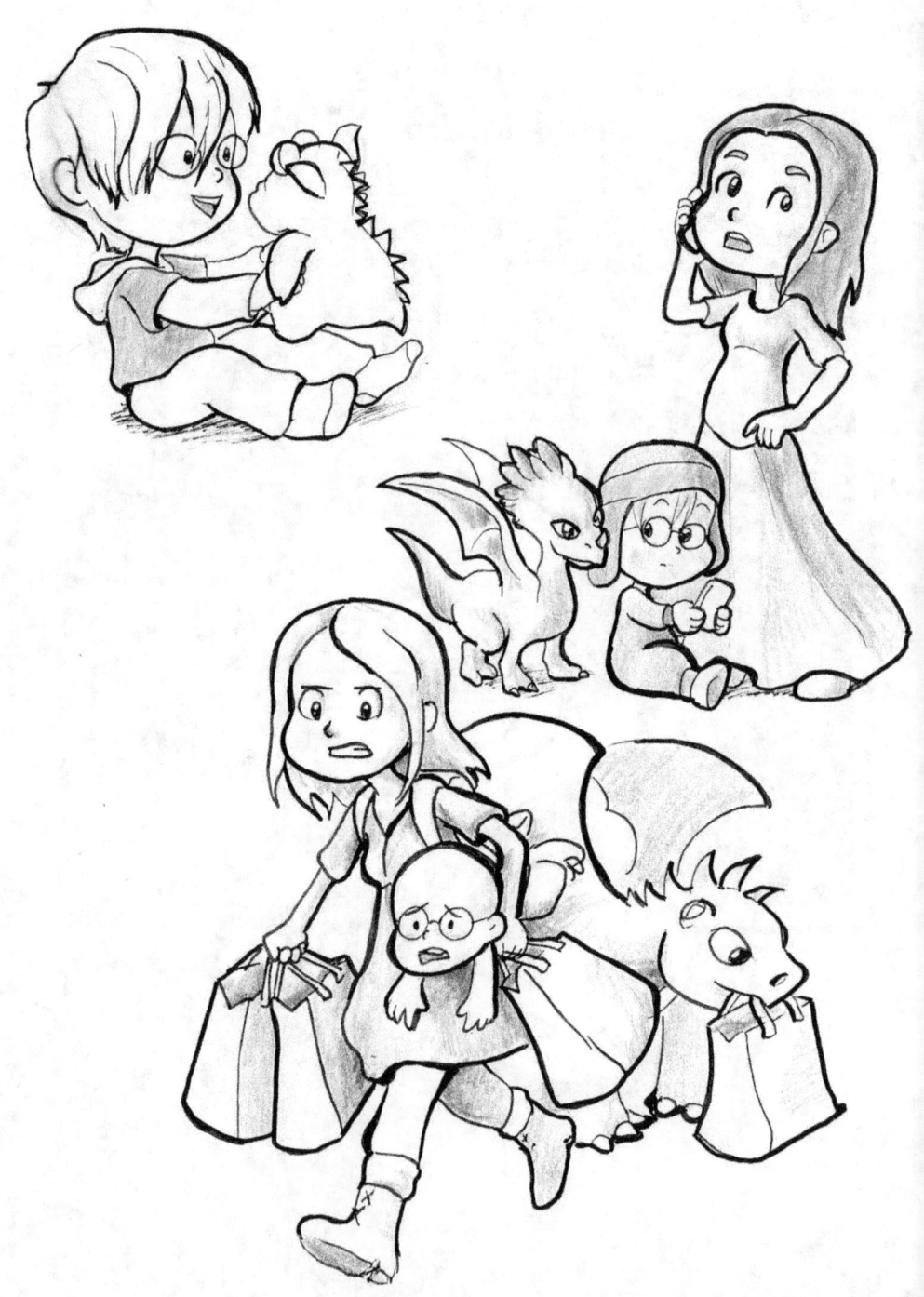

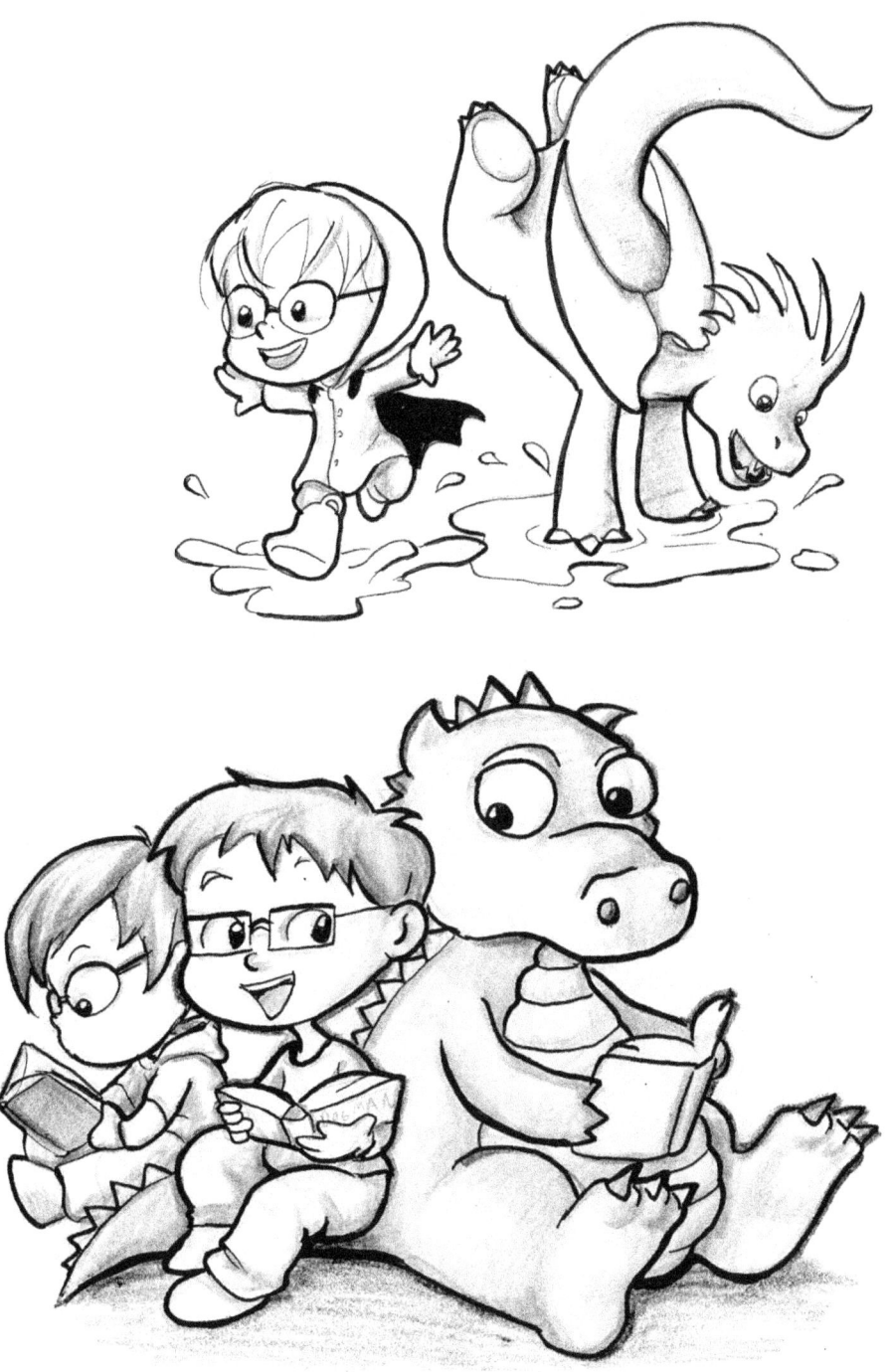

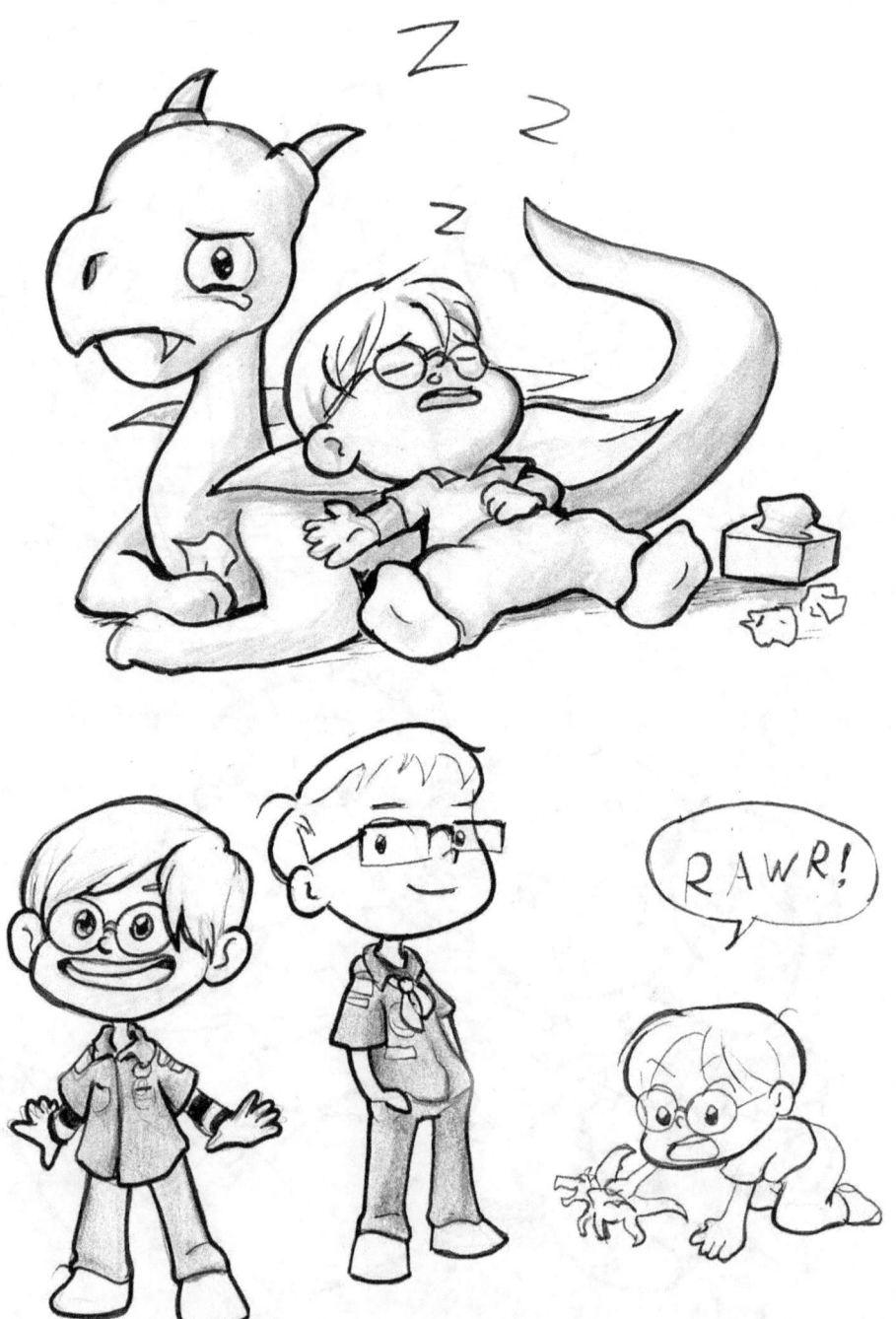

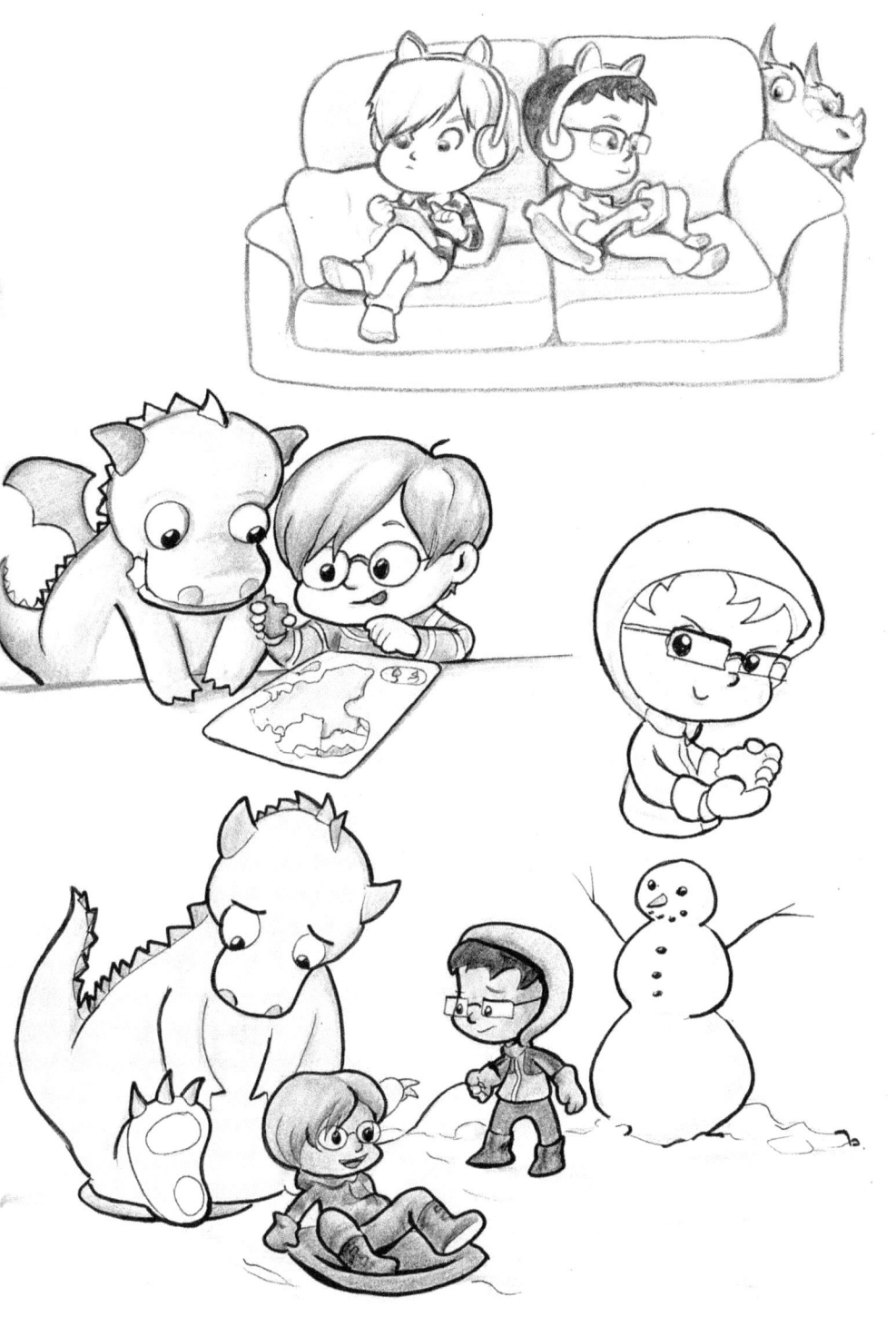

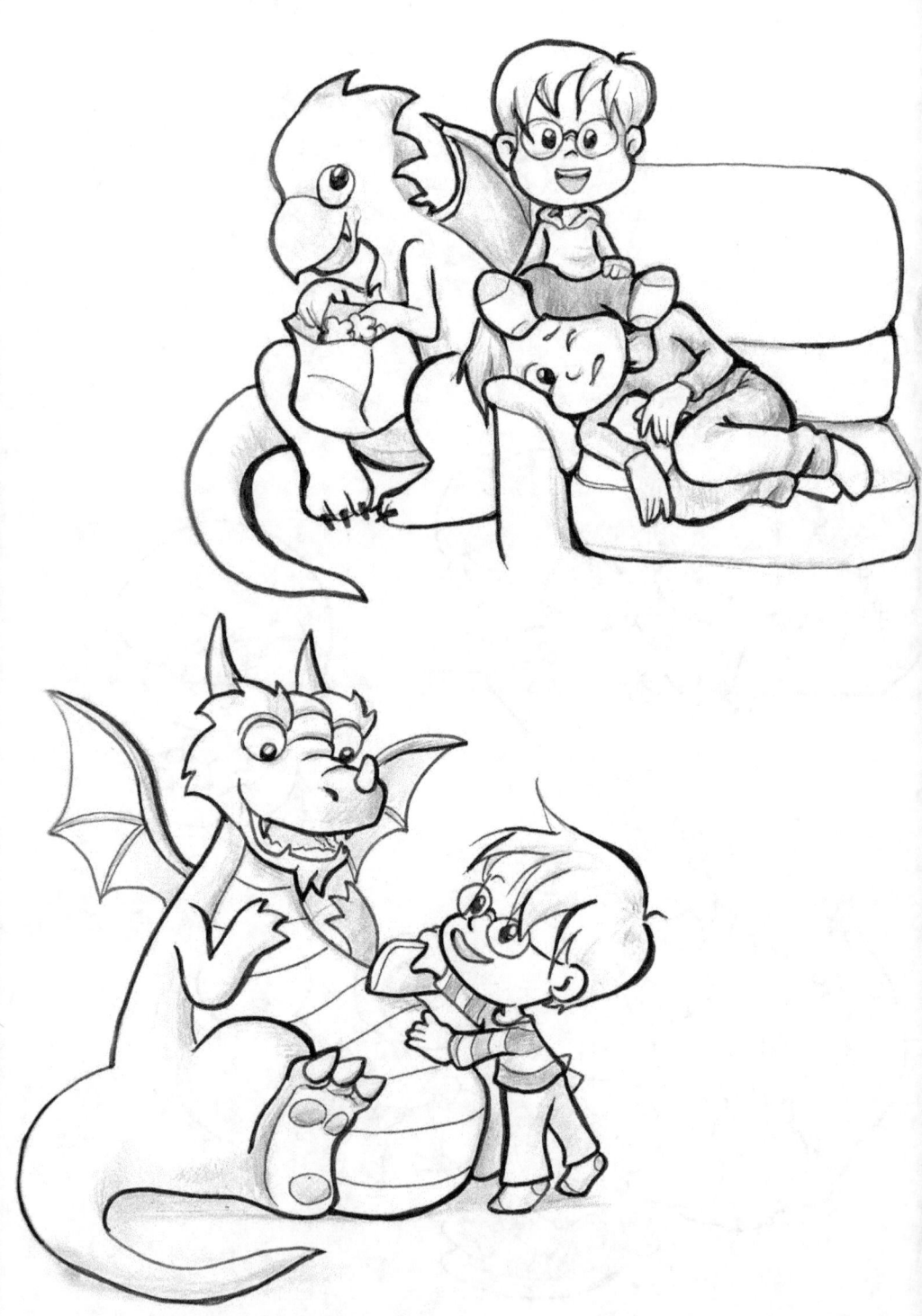

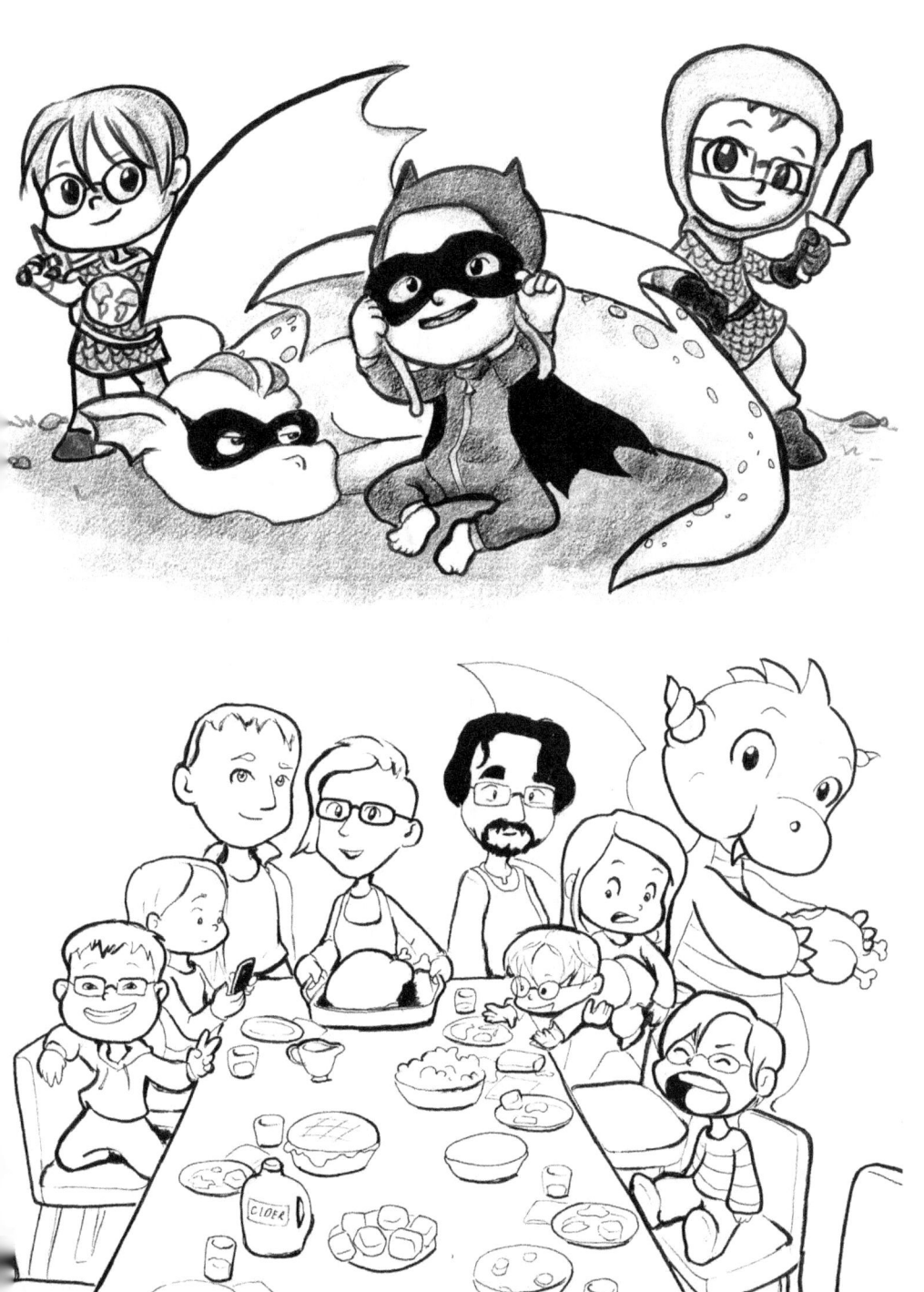

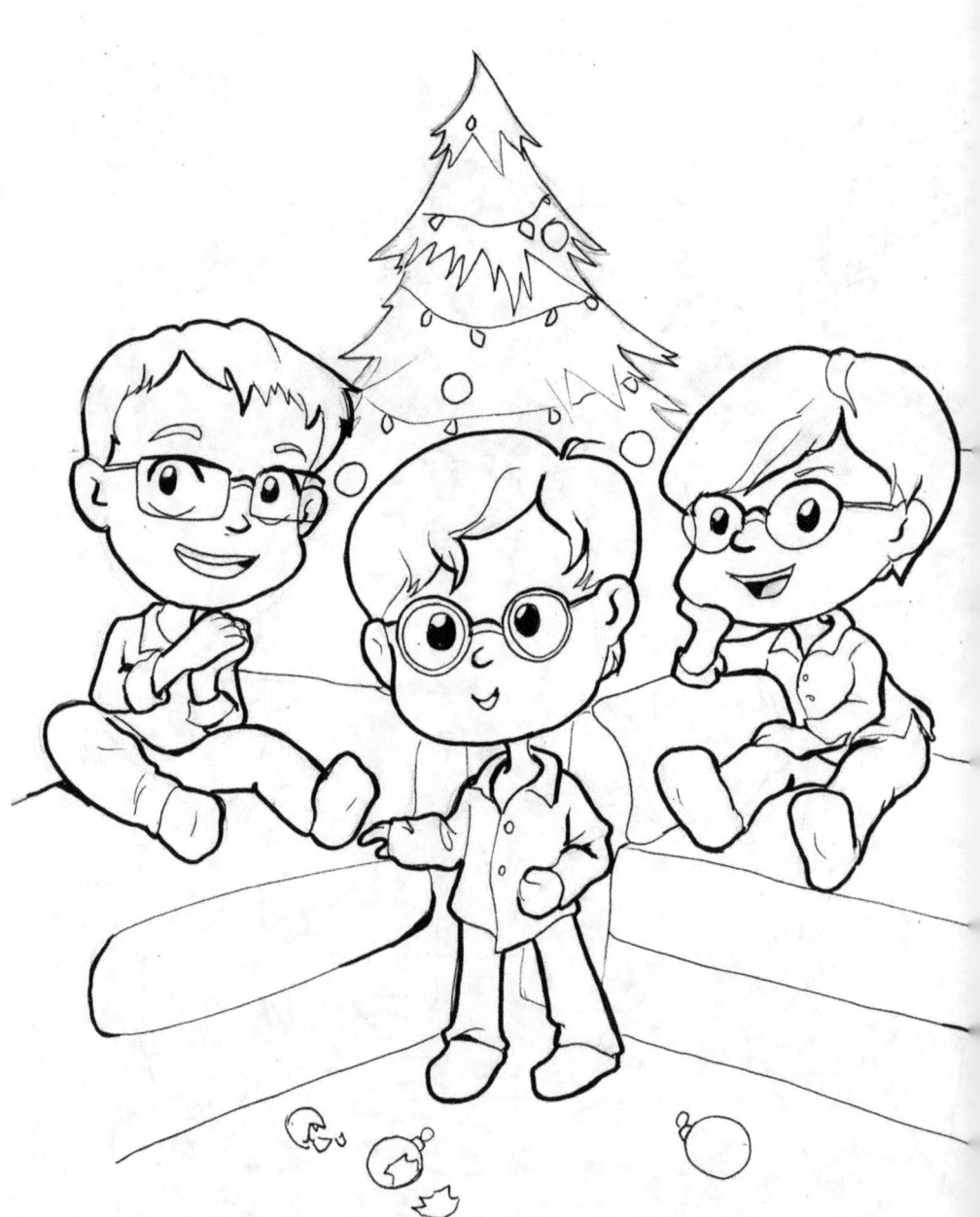

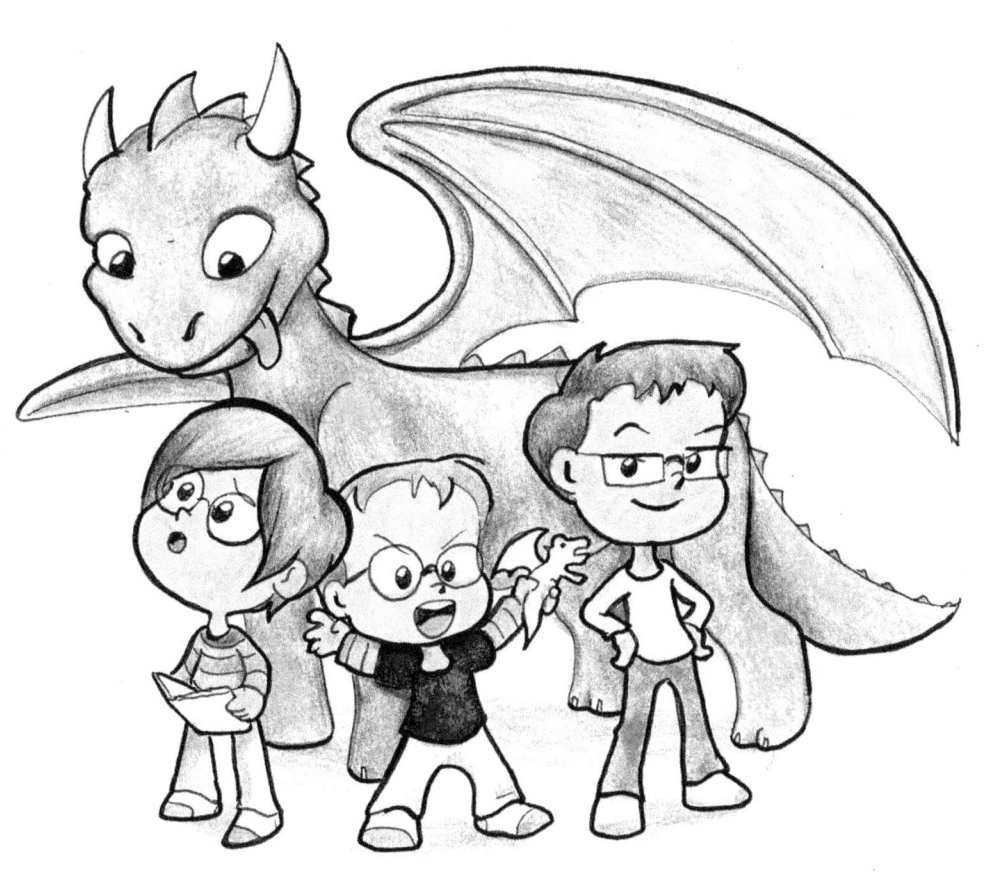

www.ingramcontent.com/pod-product-compliance
Lightning Source LLC
Chambersburg PA
CBHW051258170526
45165CB00004B/1763